5·95

084442

D0358156

THE PAST IN PERSPECTIVE

Series Editors: *C.C. Eldridge and Ralph A. Griffiths*

THE ROAD TO 1789

THE PAST IN PERSPECTIVE

Series Editors: *C.C. Eldridge and Ralph A. Griffiths*

C.C. Eldridge is Reader in History at St David's University College, Lampeter, University of Wales.

Ralph A. Griffiths is Professor of Medieval History at University College of Swansea, University of Wales.

Other titles in this series:

THE PAST IN PERSPECTIVE

THE ROAD TO 1789

FROM REFORM TO REVOLUTION
IN FRANCE

Nora Temple

CARDIFF
UNIVERSITY OF WALES PRESS
1992

British Library Cataloguing-In-Publication Data.
A catalogue record for this book is available from the British Library.

ISBN 0-7083-1144-X

Typeset by Alden Multimedia Ltd
Printed in Great Britain by Billings Book Plan Ltd., Worcester

Contents

Editors' Foreword

Each volume in this series, *The Past in Perspective*, deals with a major theme of British, European or World history. The aim of the series is to engage the interest of all for whom knowledge of the riches of the world's historical experience is a delight, and in particular to meet the needs of students of history in universities and colleges — and at comparatively modest cost.

Each theme is tackled at sufficient length and in sufficient depth to allow each writer both to advance our understanding of the subject in the light of the most recent research, and to place his or her approach in due perspective. Accordingly, each volume contains a historiographical chapter which assesses how interpretations of its theme have developed, and have been criticized, endorsed, modified or discarded. Each volume, too, includes a section of substantial excerpts from key original sources: this reflects the importance of allowing the reader to come to his or her own conclusions about differing interpretations, and also the greater accessibility nowadays of original sources in print. Furthermore, in each volume there is a detailed bibliography which not only underpins the writer's own account and analysis, but also enables the reader to pursue the theme, or particular aspects of it, to even greater depth; the explosion of historical writing in the twentieth century makes such guidance invaluable. By these perspectives, taken together, each volume is an up-to-date, authoritative and substantial exploration of themes, ancient, medieval and modern, of British, European, American and World significance, after more than a century of the study and teaching of history.

C.C. Eldridge and Ralph A. Griffiths

Explanatory note
References to the Illustrative Documents which follow the main text are indicated by a bold roman numeral preceded by the word 'DOCUMENT', all within square brackets [**DOCUMENT XII**].

1. What was the Revolution?

a) First interpretations

Understanding the French Revolution as a world historical event is a compelling challenge to every generation. The earliest and most urgent attempts to come to grips with it were undertaken by those who lived through and immediately after it, by intellectuals and politicians of a reflective mind, like Benjamin Constant, Mme de Stael, Roederer, Joseph de Maistre, and Guizot, who were driven by the need to discern the meaning of the unprecedented upheaval which dominated their lives. Their main concern was to define its nature in their terms. They saw the Revolution as a continuing process, whether they were liberals intent on rescuing the legacy of 1789 from its contaminating association with the tyranny of 1793, or radicals determined to justify 1793, or conservatives bent on demonstrating the dire consequences of abandoning tradition and following the advice of abstract thinkers. This preoccupation with the nature of the Revolution persisted for many decades because the final outcome was repeatedly thrown into question — by the Restoration, the revolutions of 1830 and 1848, and by the *coup d'état* of 1851.

Much that was written on the Revolution during these early years was prompted by, and was part of, the struggle to determine which of its political manifestations — constitutional monarchy, republic, empire — should prevail. All of these early commentaries and histories present views of the Revolution's origins. Some of them have been very influential, notably the liberal view that the Revolution was a result of the rise of the bourgeoisie, an assumption later adopted by Marx. But explaining the outbreak of the Revolution was not their main aim. Even Tocqueville, whose study of the Old Regime and the Revolution has recently acquired an unprecedented significance for some historians, was trying to explain the nature and legacy of the Revolution. His concern was to account for the France in which he lived rather than to explain why the Revolution occurred.

The current debate on the origins of the Revolution can be traced back to the consolidation of the Third Republic in the 1880s and the celebration of the first centenary of 1789. The triumph of the republicans appeared finally to mark the end of the Revolution, and it gradually stopped being a political issue and became an academic subject. The centennial itself contributed to this tranformation. One of the ways in which it was commemorated was by the endowment of chairs in Paris and some provincial universities for the study of the Revolution; another was by initiating the publication of collections of documents on the Revolution. Academic historians, whose predilection for studying the causes of events is notorious, began to give their full attention to the problem of origins. This emphasis was reinforced by the growing influence of Marxism, both as a philosophy of history and as a basis for political activism: for those who deemed the mechanism of revolution itself to be necessary to progress, particular importance inevitably attached to understanding the forces which produced this apparently outstanding example of a universal law.

b) The Marxist orthodoxy and its revision

The Marxist interpretation of the Revolution came to enjoy the status of orthodoxy for much of the twentieth century. That it did so is understandable. It incorporated much of the liberal and republican traditions. It was endorsed by a succession of distinguished French historians, notably Mathiez, Lefebvre and Soboul, whose knowledge of the Revolution, based on years of archival research, was formidable. It offered a more complete and coherent account of an intractably large and complicated subject than any alternative reading. Its central thesis, that the Revolution was a class struggle, provided a single, connected explanation of the two most perplexing issues it raised: why it occurred and why it degenerated into dictatorship. All of this was intellectually impressive and satisfying. Little wonder that Alfred Cobban's *The Social Interpretation of the Revolution* (1964), which rejected the Marxist interpretation without putting forward a well-ordered and comprehensive account in its place, was so ill received when it was first published. [**DOCUMENT I**]

Yet Cobban's book is now regularly cited as the beginning of a new phase in the historiography of the Revolution. With all its shortcomings, it prompted fresh thinking about an interpretation that had come to be taken for granted. Its main argument, that the weight of empirical research on the Revolution, including that undertaken by Lefebvre and Soboul themselves, was at variance with the Marxist conceptual framework within which it was presented, has been increasingly substantiated by subsequent studies. By the 1970s those who contested the validity of the Marxist interpretation — the 'revisionists' — were too numerous to be dismissed as Cobban had been. Their evidence was more telling than his, and the intellectual climate became more receptive to their arguments, especially in France where Marxism ceased to be the dominant intellectual force it had long been.

Its collapse was manifested in, and advanced by, François Furet's blistering attack in 1978 on the traditional Marxist reading of the Revolution. Where Mathiez had once used the Bolshevik dictatorship to justify the Jacobin, Furet condemned the Terror by equating it with Stalin's Gulag. A mood which might almost be described as anti-Marxist triumphalism emerged in the 1980s, encouraged by the decline of the French Communist Party and the discrediting and collapse of communism in Eastern Europe and the Soviet Union. By the time of the bicentennial celebrations, reaction against the Marxist interpretation of the Revolution had even produced a growing scepticism about the Revolution itself. The official celebration of the Declaration of the Rights of Man was accompanied by much discussion in the media that was often dismissive of the Revolution. Many of the classic conservative arguments against it were repeated: it had cut short a promising effort by the Old Regime to reform itself, it had handicapped the modernization of the French economy, it had given birth to a political tradition which led to twentieth-century totalitarianism. This scepticism underlay a new general interpretation of the Revolution, largely inspired by Furet and his rediscovery of Tocqueville's reading of the Revolution. This was most fully manifested in a massive academic and publishing enterprise promoted to coincide with, though not to commemorate, still less to celebrate, the bicentennial.

Anything now written on the Revolution is bound to reflect, and to reflect upon, the turmoil of the past three decades in the historiography of the Revolution — the critique of the Marxist interpretation and the alternative readings offered by those who have been described as the 'soft revisionists', of whom Cobban himself might be seen as a representative figure, and those dubbed the 'hard revisionists', led by Furet. What then is understood by 'the Marxist interpretation' and the varieties of 'revisionism'?

In the Marxist interpretation, the Revolution was a class conflict, a struggle for power between a reactionary nobility and a progressive bourgeoisie. It was the result not of political or climatic contingencies, of impending bankruptcy, maladroit leadership, or harvest failure, but rather of structural change and contradiction. The change was the rise of an emergent capitalist bourgeoisie, which by the late eighteenth century was the dominant economic force in France; the contradiction lay in its being denied political power by a feudal nobility, the dominant social class. Cut off by its values and social prejudices from the new commercial and industrial sources of wealth, the nobility was all the more determined to retain control of the state. For this reason, it had to be removed from its position as a privileged élite. A quarrel between the monarchy and the nobility gave the bourgeoisie the chance to overthrow the Old Regime in 1789. The new progressive class triumphed thanks to the support of the lower classes in town and country, and its success launched the industrial capitalism of the nineteenth century. One of the strengths of this interpretation is its comprehensive nature: the conflict between nobility and bourgeoisie explains not only the early liberal phase of the Revolution but also the Jacobin dictatorship and government by Terror in 1793–4. This is seen as an aberration, forced on the revolutionary leadership by the need to defend the liberal achievement of 1789 from attack by counter-revolutionary forces at home and abroad. The other great merit of the Marxist interpretation is that it is consistent with the revolutionaries' own sense of being involved in an event of world historical importance, in which men emancipated themselves from the past, seized control of their destiny, and inaugurated a new era for mankind.

What undermined the Marxist interpretation and led George V. Taylor, a leading American authority on the Revolution, to proclaim confidently in 1979 that the class-struggle thesis had expired was the impossibility of accommodating within it the findings of empirical research. It was one of Cobban's enduring achievements that he was the first to point this out. Much of the evidence he used against the Marxist interpretation was drawn from the work of Marxist historians themselves. In *The Social Interpretation of the French Revolution* he dismissed the three main features of the Marxist scenario by drawing attention to what was in fact already well established: that the economy and society of France had long ceased to be feudal by 1789; that the revolutionary leadership was recruited not from an emerging capitalist class but from landowners, lawyers, and other members of the middle-class professions; and that, far from stimulating industrial take-off in France, the Revolution actually hampered it. He also questioned whether popular revolutionary movements had pursued the same goals as the bourgeois revolution, an assumption essential to the Marxist interpretation because it was the actions of the urban and rural lower classes which thwarted military repression in 1789 and gave the Revolution its radical character. Subsequent research confirmed and amplified Cobban's demolition of the Marxist interpretation, though not the alternative hypotheses he tentatively put forward.

Cobban's book was followed by a stream of articles and monographs probing the Marxist interpretation. Most of them focused on the origins of the Revolution, particularly the nature of, and relations between, the nobility and bourgeoisie. These proved to have been not at all the clearly differentiated social classes, based on diametrically opposed economic interests, postulated by the Marxists. Both categories were divided internally and they overlapped. The nobility included familiar types — court aristocrats and country gentry, landlords (large and small), judges, holders of venal offices in the royal administration, and army officers — but also, unexpectedly, financiers, shipowners, sugar-refiners, coal and iron-masters. On the other hand, the bourgeoisie included landlords (large and small), judges, holders of venal offices in the royal administration, as well as financiers, shipowners, sugar-refiners, coal and iron-masters, textile merchants, lawyers and doctors. This diversity and the indeterminacy of class boundaries resulted from the openness of French society under the Old Regime: it was hierarchical, but noble status was readily accessible to wealthy commoners who could make their way to the top by purchasing ennobling offices. The goal of the successful financier, merchant and manufacturer was to join, not overthrow, the nobility, which is why they invested in traditional forms of property — land, *rentes*, offices — as soon as they could afford to do so.

This process accounts for the enduring vigour of the nobility: it was continually refreshed by injections of non-noble talent and wealth. Prejudice against what were once regarded as dishonourable pursuits was eroded. Bourgeois who acquired nobility in the eighteenth century often remained in business, while members of the old nobility took it up. Nobles and bourgeois met on equal terms in provincial academies and masonic lodges and were equally receptive to enlightened ideas critical of authoritarian government. There was rampant snobbery in the upper reaches of French society, but this in itself is evidence of upward social mobility: long-established members of an élite can manifest their disdain only if they meet *nouveaux-riches* and *arrivistes* socially. It has been suggested that upward social mobility may have become more difficult in the late eighteenth century as a result of the increase in population and wealth, but most of the evidence does not bear this out. Indeed the latest research, by David D. Bien on the purchase of the venal office of *secrétaire du roi*, one of the most efficient if expensive ways of attaining hereditary nobility, reveals that the high tide of ennoblement by this means came not in the seventeenth century, as is often supposed, but after 1730, when between 900 and 1,000 new nobles and their families joined the legal élite each generation by this pecuniary method alone.

Belief in economic retardation under the Old Regime was destroyed even earlier than belief in a hidebound, reactionary nobility. F. Crouzet demonstrated, in a path-breaking essay published in 1967, that the French economy as a whole expanded at about the same rate as that of Britain in the eighteenth century. There was significant growth in the production of traditional textiles such as wool, linen and silk, a dramatic expansion of the new cotton textiles, and a spectacular fivefold (threefold if allowance is made for inflation) increase in overseas trade. There were weaknesses in the performance of the French economy: agricultural output more or less kept pace with the growth in population, but there was little margin to spare; the increase in manufactures was achieved by expanding existing methods of production, not by introducing more efficient techniques; and overseas trade was too dependent on the import and re-export of colonial products. On the other hand, royal ministers were neither blind to, nor complacent about, these shortcomings, and tried to stimulate improvements in both agriculture and industry. The economy went into recession in the late 1770s, but opinion is divided as to whether this was a sign of inherent structural weakness or just a transitional adjustment to rapid expansion. Crouzet's verdict on the prospects of the pre-revolutionary French economy remains as favourable after two decades of further research as it was in 1967.

c) *Post-Marxist views*

Finding fault with the Marxist interpretation was easier than finding an acceptable alternative to put in its place, or even escaping from all its assumptions. The idea that the Revolution was fuelled by social tension was difficult to throw off. Cobban failed to do so. He replaced conflict between nobles and bourgeois with conflict between notables (landlords, lawyers, officialdom) and lower orders, a substitution which commanded little support. Colin Lucas also jettisoned Marxist categories but continued to postulate a crucial role for social tension. He pointed to the resentment of those who had made it to the top among those who had not quite done so; this became increasingly important as population growth increased pressure on available channels of social advancement. A similar conclusion was reached by Robert Darnton. He attributed the scabrous radicalism of pre-revolutionary pamphleteering and journalism to the frustrations of a new and larger generation of would-be Voltaires, Brissot being the most notorious, who turned to the gutter press for a living because the literary patronage available was not sufficient to provide for all those who aspired to make their way as men of letters. Sarah Maza has described those who persist with the belief that tension somewhere in society, if not between nobles and bourgeois, was responsible for the Revolution as the 'soft revisionists'. None of them has filled the gap left by the collapse of the Marxist interpretation because none of them has produced evidence of a social conflict capable of explaining both the political crisis which destroyed the Old Regime and the struggle for power which dominated the Revolution.

'Hard revisionists', to continue with Maza's categories, are those who have concluded from the collapse of the Marxist scenario that all social interpretations are suspect and have instead opted for a political reading of the Revolution. The most radical of 'hard revisionists' is Furet, whose view of the Revolution has dominated academic debate, at least in terms of the controversy aroused, since it was first put forward in *Penser la Révolution Française* in 1978 (translated as *Interpreting the French Revolution*, 1981). It also informs some of the most important scholarly publications to appear at the time of the bicentennial, notably *A Critical Dictionary of the French Revolution* (1989) and the three volumes of conference papers published under the general title *The French Revolution and the Creation of Modern Political Culture* (1987, 1988, 1989).

Furet's inspiration is Tocqueville, who concluded in the mid nineteenth century that the Revolution had had little impact on the society and economy of France. Furet was also impressed by Tocqueville's insistence that historians must distinguish between what happened in the past and what those who were involved believed to have happened. Whereas the revolutionaries believed they had effected a radical break with the past and created a new society and state, Tocqueville was convinced that their real achievement was to have continued and completed the work of administrative centralization initiated by the Bourbon monarchy. Administrative centralization was to Tocqueville's view of the Revolution what the class struggle was to Marx's — a total explanation of its origins, nature and achievement. He believed that the centralizing effort of the monarchy was responsible for the Revolution because it deprived the French people of political responsibility; as a result they accepted uncritically the abstract, impractical ideas of the Enlightenment and repudiated the Old Regime because it did not live up to them. It was these same utopian ideas, combined with the political immaturity of the revolutionaries, which prevented them from creating a stable new regime. The persistence of revolutionary instability let in the Jacobins and enabled them to restore administrative centralization in an infinitely more oppressive form than that of the Old Regime.

Tocqueville arrived at this interpretation of the Revolution from the perspective of the Second Empire. *The Old Regime and the French Revolution* was first published in 1856, when it was reasonable to identify the Revolution with the consummation of administrative centralization. Furet qualified and developed Tocqueville's insight in reaction against the Bolshevik Revolution and Soviet dictatorship. It is important to remember that his is the thesis of a former Marxist, formulated during the terminal convulsions of Marxism as the dominant intellectual force in France. Furet's conclusion is that while the Revolution certainly completed the administrative centralization of the Old Regime, its main achievement was to have inaugurated modern political culture. It broke with the past by establishing a new basis for political legitimacy — democratic egalitarianism or the Will of the People, the most radical of the abstract ideas promoted by the *philosophes*. He believes that the triumph of this principle over rival concepts such as individual rights, the rule of law, liberalism, and political pluralism was assured by the Revolution of 1789 and led inexorably first to war, then to dictatorship.

Furet's view of the origins of the Revolution was refined and tested at a conference held in Chicago in September 1986. The papers delivered at that conference were published the following year, edited by Keith Michael Baker, under the title *The Political Culture of the Old Regime*, the first of three volumes published under the general title of *The French Revolution and the Creation of Modern Political Culture*. The majority of these papers present evidence which bears out Furet's claims; but several do not, and the strength of some of the favourable evidence is open to question. The plausibility of Furet's interpretation depends on two salient points: the character of relations between the monarchy and corporate society, and the strength of support for political ideas which might broadly be described as Rousseauist in 1789.

The relationship between monarchy, corporate bodies and the rest of society was not as clear-cut as Tocqueville suggested. The power of the Crown undoubtedly increased from the sixteenth century, and at the same time the monarch himself became increasingly cut off from the nation by the instruments of that power, the court at Versailles and the centralized bureaucratic administration. Corporate bodies — law courts, provincial estates, town councils — survived, but their independence was constrained by the royal council and the intendants. But though their capacity to defend and represent their localities and assist the Crown was diminished, it did not disappear altogether. They provided the Crown with credit and played an indispensable role in local administration; they were the only institutional curbs on authoritarianism; and their opposition to the Crown was as often prompted by public opinion as by self-interest.

The symbiotic nature of the relationship between Crown and corporate bodies was demonstrated when that relationship was breached by Maupeou's attack on the parlements in 1770–1, which turned out to be as damaging to the monarchy as to the parlements themselves. It confirmed fears that absolutism was inherently despotic and that ultimately the parlements were impotent, dependent on the complacency or weakness of the government for such constitutional restraints as they were able to exert. By revealing that there were no effective limits on royal power, Maupeou provoked the most urgent political debate since the Fronde, and prompted demands that the Estates-General be summoned.

The nature of this debate is of crucial importance to Furet's interpretation. The received opinion is that the case against absolutism before the Revolution, largely inspired by Montesquieu and the parlementary cause, was dominated by concepts such as individual rights, equality before the law (but not necessarily political equality), the rule of law and the separation of powers, all of which might be described as liberal; while more radical, democratic concepts, such as political equality and the general will, usually associated with Rousseau, became influential only during the course of the Revolution. The Chicago conference was presented with evidence, mostly derived from political tracts, that the more radical concepts were very much more influential before 1789 than previously believed, and that they had swept all before them in 1789 as a result of the elections to the Estates-General and the attempt of the nobility to maintain its political predominance. This is in line with Tocqueville's conclusion that the reason for the Revolution and its dire outcome was that public opinion in France fell under the sway of men of ideas devoid of experience of public affairs. Yet other evidence, derived from studies of the parlements, provincial academies and masonic lodges, suggests that there was still considerable support for liberalism before 1789. What happened during and in the years immediately after 1789 supports the conclusion that political opinion, far from being dominated by democratic egalitarianism, constituted a spectrum. This is borne out not simply by the Declaration of the Rights of Man, which included liberal principles of government (individual rights, the rule of law, the separation of powers) alongside more democratic concepts of popular sovereignty and equality, but also by the liberal phase of the Revolution, which lasted until 1792.

Furet's perspective on the Revolution is dominated by the Terror. He takes the failure of constitutional monarchy for granted. The Marxist version of determinism has been relinquished, but not determinism itself. The result, a neat schematic interpretation of the Revolution, is achieved by starting with a very narrow definition of what has to be explained.

d) The present perspective

The discussion which follows reflects different conclusions about the Revolution and its origins. Though the Revolution was an essentially political event, it had social and economic causes, repercussions and consequences which were significant, even if their significance was not that set out in the Marxist interpretation. There was discontinuity in much more than political ideology and culture between the Old Regime and the new revolutionary order. And the political outcome of the Revolution is more accurately described by the plural 'cultures' than the singular 'culture'.

The origins of the Revolution will be located in the political structures, policies and politics of the Old Regime. It occurred because in 1788 the monarchy was forced to abandon absolutism. It had tried for about three decades and with very limited success to introduce the major reforms that were deemed necessary if France was to maintain its international ascendancy. It discovered that radical changes in the financing and administration of the state could not be achieved without equally radical changes in its political structures. But the basis and *raison d'être* of the Old Regime was stability. That stability was achieved by Louis XIV after the mid-seventeenth-century crisis, not because the state triumphed over corporate society, but because it compromised with it. The Crown asserted its right to determine state policy — national representative bodies like the Estates-General and the Assembly of Notables fell into disuse — but it respected most surviving administrative and social institutions. The nobility accepted the loss of independent political power but retained its privileged social status; the parlements acquiesced in the political docility that Louis XIV required of them, while he gave up all efforts to reform the judiciary; the intendants exercised a tutelage over the provincial estates, town councils, *bureaux des finances* and *élections*, but had to work through them.

There was very little scope for any but minor changes within this compromise; it could certainly not accommodate the reforms sought by the Crown in the second half of the eighteenth century, precisely because they threatened the survival of corporate bodies and legal orders whose complacency was essential to the functioning of the supposedly absolute monarchy. This is why attacks on them, like Maupeou's reform of the parlements and Calonne's attempt to reform taxation, provoked a clamour for the revival of the old representative institutions. Absolutism was tolerated so long as the Crown recognized that there were in practice strict limits to the sovereignty which the concept of divine-right monarchy assigned to it.

Corporate bodies like the parlements were able to mobilize popular support because the first reforms introduced by the Crown coincided with the persecution of the Jansenists in the 1750s, which permanently damaged the monarchy's reputation. Other reforms were associated with bankruptcy and flagrant breaches of the rule of law by royal ministers. When the Crown at length recognized that the changes it sought could not be achieved within existing authoritarian structures, it lost control over the transition to new, more representative ones. A cumulative series of tactical misjudgements gave rise to a disastrous political and social confrontation during the weeks immediately before and after the meeting of the Estates-General. Opinion was polarized and the stakes raised: either military repression or a new regime more radical than it need otherwise have been would result. What finally ensured that 1789 was not just a repetition of the Fronde, that there would indeed be a new regime, and that it would be radical, was the intervention of the popular classes. The end of the Old Regime was a result of its inherent structural weakness. The Revolution was born of contingency, of the coincidence in 1788 of decisions as to how the Estates-General was to be composed and elected with the failure of the harvest and all its consequent privations and disorder.

2. The Depredations of War and Debt

In 1744, when Louis XV seemed to be dying, private individuals paid for 6,000 masses to be said at Notre-Dame for the recovery of a king who was still evidently 'the well-beloved' of his subjects. In 1757, when his life was again thought to be in danger after Damiens stabbed him, 600 masses were requested. In 1774, when he was indeed dying, only three masses were said for him and there was open rejoicing in Paris when his demise was announced. This reaction, though harsh, is not surprising given Louis's mounting unpopularity during the last quarter-century of his reign. After he took personal charge of government in 1743 following the death of Fleury, his former tutor and chief minister, its record had been a catalogue of disasters. Two long expensive wars brought France nothing but defeat and humiliation. There were incessant battles with the parlements over religion and taxation. Dramatic changes in economic policy and local government were introduced and quickly jettisoned. Partial bankruptcy and an attack on the judiciary, perceived to be the last safeguard against despotism, in the last years of Louis XV's reign ensured that his death would not be regretted.

The discredit incurred by one king does not necessarily damage the institution of monarchy itself, and the events that immediately followed Louis XV's death might be taken as evidence that his unpopularity was personal and all that was needed to restore the prestige of the Crown was new leadership and a fresh direction. Louis XVI and Marie Antoinette were greeted enthusiastically on their accession. Public rejoicing increased when Mme du Barry, the late king's mistress, was confined to a convent, his more notorious ministers were sacked, and the policies associated with them reversed. None the less the conclusion that emerges from recent research on the middle decades of the eighteenth century is that the events of the twenty-five years before Louis XV's death were critical in preparing the way for the Revolution. They undermined the complex political and social compromise between royal absolutism and corporate rights

on which the Old Regime was founded and they defined and gave
public currency to the ideas which dominated political discourse and
decisions during the Revolution.

If these setbacks had been followed by a generation of quiet recuper-
ation, such as France enjoyed after the disasters of Louis XIV's last
years and the turbulence of the Regency, it is conceivable that they
might now be seen as passing misfortunes. What made them the
beginning of the end was the government's decision to seek revenge
for earlier defeats abroad. A foreign policy motivated by the desire to
demonstrate the international ascendancy of France drew it into a
third ill-considered and expensive war, that for American independence. This led to the last financial crisis of the Old Regime, a crisis
which could not be resolved within the existing political structures.

War played a major role in undermining the Old Regime. This is
not surprising. War was one of the chief activities of the states of early
modern Europe, an accepted way of achieving international goals and
a source of matchless prestige if crowned with victory. None had
responded more vigorously to the challenge of organizing and
financing war than the Bourbon dynasty. In the seventeenth century
its efforts to improve the country's military effectiveness imposed a
crippling burden on the French economy, but at least the territory of
France was enlarged and its frontiers strengthened. These gains might
have been achieved at less cost, to both royal finances and France's
alliances and international standing, if Mazarin and Louis XIV had
not at times given way to arrogance, but there can be no doubt of the
strategic value of the territory acquired. This was amply demonstrated in Louis XIV's last two wars when France was for several
years able to withstand attack from all sides by the armies of a general
European coalition.

a) Policy and geography

The wars of the eighteenth century brought no comparable material
gain to France. The sole exception was the short, limited and, from
the French point of view, very successful war over the Polish succession (1733–5/8). France went to war to uphold the election which
should have conferred the Polish throne on Louis XV's father-in-law,
Stanislas Leszczynski. It did not achieve this aim — indeed in the
event it made little real effort to do so — but by way of compensation
it secured for him the duchy of Lorraine, with the proviso that it

would revert to the French Crown on his death. This outcome could hardly have been better for France. which had long sought possession of Lorraine. Its assimilation completed the consolidation of the eastern frontier.

The next two wars, the War of Austrian Succession (1740–8) and the Seven Years War (1756–63), present the sharpest possible contrast. Fought in Europe, North America, the West Indies, the Mediterranean and India, they were long, expensive, and ended in humiliating defeat and the loss of the greater part of French overseas possessions. The cause of these disasters is often located in the geography of France, which placed it at a grave strategic disadvantage compared with its rivals, Britain and the German states. The argument runs that because France was a continental power with a long Atlantic coast, it was unable to concentrate either on land war or on colonial and commercial expansion, but was obliged instead to pursue both simultaneously. Coalitions between its continental and maritime rivals — Britain and Austria in the War of Austrian Succession, Britain and Prussia in the Seven Years War — resulted in the multi-theatre wars of the mid eighteenth century. These over-stretched French resources and led to defeat nearly everywhere.

This geopolitical and deterministic view is founded on two questionable premises. The first is that further expansion on the Continent at the expense of the German powers was feasible for France; the second is that wars fought simultaneously in Europe and in America could not be kept separate. Cardinal Fleury, who had a better grasp of the international interests of France than any other eighteenth-century minister, subscribed to neither premise. He recognized that once France had acquired the reversionary right to Lorraine, it could make no more significant territorial gains on the Continent that would be tolerated by the other powers. He believed that France should therefore concentrate on expanding its overseas commerce, which is why securing trading concessions for French merchants was always a major aim of his diplomacy and one that was pursued with considerable success while he was chief minister (1726–43). His ultimate goal was to wrest from Britain the advantages it enjoyed in trade with Spain's colonies, not just those formally conceded by the Treaty of Utrecht but also the more valuable contraband trade that flourished behind the legal concessions. To achieve this Fleury cultivated good relations with Spain and improved the size and quality of the French navy. In August 1740 he dispatched the Brest and Toulon fleets to the

West Indies to fight alongside Spain in the Anglo-Spanish war that
had started the previous year.

   Fleury held to his strategy of concentrating on the struggle in the
Caribbean even after the death of Charles VI of Austria in October
1740, and he did his utmost to prevent France from joining the
coalition that was developing in central Europe against Charles VI's
daughter, Maria Theresa. If France specifically refrained from
attacking the Austrian Netherlands, then Dutch neutrality was
probable and that of Hanover might be secured. France was certainly
well able to remain on the defensive in Europe, given the strength of
its land frontiers, and if it had done so Britain would have had neither
the occasion nor the opportunity to intervene on the Continent. In the
event, France joined the coalition against Austria. Louis XV was
persuaded by Belle-Isle, Chauvelin and other leaders of France's
military aristocracy (who had for some time been chafing against
Fleury's prudent and peaceful policy) that the challenge to Maria
Theresa by Prussia and Bavaria presented France with a golden
opportunity to triumph over its traditional enemy. The European and
American struggles were thus fused, not as a result of the constraints
of geography but because of ill-judged policy decisions.

b) Mistakes and confusions

The War of Austrian Succession, which was meant to be a short and
sharp campaign to dismember Austria, turned into a calamity for
France. French armies led by Saxe won a succession of victories
against Austrian forces in the Netherlands. But this was terrain which
Austria made little effort to defend, knowing that the British and the
Dutch would veto France's retention of it at the end of the war. The
campaigns in Germany and Italy went badly for France, partly
because its allies, Prussia and Spain, were unreliable, and partly
because there was no clear sense of purpose behind French policy.
Much of the blame for this rests with the king, who took personal
charge of the direction of government after Fleury's death in 1743.
Louis XV, who was easily bored by the daily grind of government
business, found it difficult to make and maintain clear policy
decisions.

   The king's vacillation and weakness for intrigue and personal diplomacy were exploited by court factions urging rival foreign policy
strategies behind the backs of royal ministers. But the root cause of

this confusion was the absence of a tangible objective that France had any prospect of securing by means of continental war. France found itself fighting to aggrandize Prussia and Spain because, as Fleury had grasped, there were no territorial gains France could make in Europe that would be internationally acceptable. Weakening Austria might be in the French interest, but this did not require the participation of France in the anti-Habsburg coalition. Unable to concentrate its resources on the colonial front, France was defeated in North America and the West Indies. Seven years of fighting involving heavy loss of resources ended in stalemate and, apart from some minor gains in India, a return to the *status quo ante bellum*. Public regard for Louis XV was badly undermined: contemporary opinion is reflected in the scornful description of the Treaty of Aix-la-Chapelle as 'the peace which passeth all understanding', because, despite Saxe's many triumphs, it brought France nothing.

Louis XV might be forgiven for his part in the first of these two multi-theatre conflicts — he was inexperienced and had not been properly trained by Fleury — but it is more difficult to find extenuating reasons for French involvement in the second. The Seven Years War was not sought by France. On the contrary, Louis XV and his ministers were intent on preserving peace so as to restore the Crown's finances. But to suggest that they were the unwitting victims of the ambitions of British colonists in North America and of the machinations of the Austrian Chancellor Kaunitz in Europe is also to suggest that French diplomacy was incompetent. Some allowance has to be made for the slowness of communications across the Atlantic, which made it difficult to keep up with, let alone control, events in North America. Largely as a result of this, Britain and France became involved in a struggle which neither wanted for the Ohio valley. But if bad luck explains the renewal of the war between Britain and France, it cannot account for the fact that France simultaneously became embroiled in yet another European conflict from which it had nothing to gain. That it did so was the result of poor judgement on the part of Louis XV.

His intemperate reaction to the news that his ally, Frederick of Prussia, had signed the Convention of Westminster with Britain in January 1756 allowed Kaunitz to trap him into an alliance with Austria and a rerun of the struggle for Silesia, though this time France was on the Austrian, not the Prussian, side. The Convention came as a surprise, and caused offence, because Frederick had neither consulted nor warned the French government about his move. Yet the undertaking he gave Britain that he would guarantee the neutrality of Hanover if war broke out between Britain and France was consistent with French policy to avoid becoming embroiled in the Austro-Prussian war that was about to break out in central Europe. Frederick in effect provided France with an excellent opportunity to resume Fleury's strategy of excluding Britain from the Continent so as to concentrate on the colonial struggle brewing in North America. Ill-feeling existed between Britain and both of its continental allies, Austria and the Dutch Republic. Their neutrality could be assured if France respected the integrity of Austria's territory, notably the Netherlands, which it had no realistic prospect of acquiring anyway. Unfortunately, relations between Louis and Frederick were such as to prevent the French king taking a detached view of the Convention of Westminster and the potential advantage to France of Hanoverian neutrality. Prussia's agreement with Britain aroused indignation because it presumed to impose limits on the freedom of action of Europe's leading power, France. Kaunitz was able to exploit this irrational resentment to push Louis into a *rapprochement* with Austria, negotiated behind the backs of his ministers who thought that the alliance with Prussia was essential to France's interests.

Louis did not intend to commit France to supporting Austria in a war to restore Habsburg power in Italy and Germany, but that was the upshot of his ill-considered initiative. The French found themselves fielding a large army in Europe and paying Austria an annual war subsidy in return for nothing more substantial than the prospect of a small part of the Austrian Netherlands at the end of the war as their reward. Because of its continental commitments, France was once again unable to give its armies in the colonies the support they needed, and this led to defeat in North America, the West Indies, and India. It ought to have been able to count on the support of Spain, and a joint effort by Spain and France in the Caribbean and western Mediterranean from 1756 would have improved the chances of both countries of recovering what they had lost to Britain since 1713. But Spain remained neutral until 1761. Its stance was partly a response to the Austro-French alliance, which Spain viewed as inimical to its chance of extending its own territory in Italy; partly it resulted from the personal animus towards France of the Spanish queen, Barbara, who was Portuguese and pro-British. Relations between France and Spain improved after the death of Ferdinand VI. His successor, Charles III, signed an alliance in 1761 with France to recover Gibraltar and exclude British trade from central America, but by that time France was exhausted. Spain's late entry into the war simply permitted Britain to deal with its most dangerous naval rivals piecemeal.

France could expect no help from Austria and Russia in the naval and colonial conflict — the divergence between its aims and those of its allies in this war was even more marked than in the previous one — and it was less than half-hearted in the backing it gave them in east-central Europe. Louis XV viewed the recovery of Austria and the expansion of Russia with mounting concern because their growing strength was a threat to the security of France's old allies, Sweden, Poland, and the Ottoman Empire. The king's animosity towards Russia frustrated repeated attempts by his foreign ministers, Bernis and Choiseul, to get that state, which was not at war with Britain, to mediate a general peace settlement. Louis was not prepared to pay Russia's price for mediation — acquiescence in its expansion in eastern Europe — and he conspired with his ambassadors in Warsaw and St Petersburg to subvert his ministers' instructions. It could be said that France sacrificed a substantial cause, North America, for an illusory one, Polish independence.

c) The costs of war

The war resulted in massive loss of territory, not just in North America, but also in India, West Africa, and the West Indies. This was not as damaging as comparable losses might have been to Britain. France remained the single most powerful state in Europe with vast resources in manpower and wealth, though its future as a colonial power was limited, with all that this implied for its long-term economic development. However, persuasive evidence has been put forward by James C. Riley that the immediate impact of the Seven Years War on France's overseas trade was not as disastrous as is usually thought. What probably hurt more at the time was the public damage to France's international prestige. Its navy was trounced by the British. Its armies in Germany, along with those of Austria and Russia, failed to defeat Prussia, a relatively minor power. (The population of Prussia was 3.5 million whereas the combined population of France, Austria and Russia was 70 million.) Frederick the Great's astonishing military successes were openly admired in Paris. Little wonder that the alliance with Austria was regarded with such loathing in France, and that there was such prejudice against Marie Antoinette, who married Louis XV's grandson in 1770 and was the living embodiment of that alliance.

Worst of all were the domestic consequences, financial and political. France could afford the War of Austrian Succession, which cost an average of 90–100 million *livres* per year, according to the estimates of Riley, but not the second, very much more expensive, war a few years later. The average annual cost of the Seven Years War was over 200 million *livres*. This necessitated large-scale borrowing on unfavourable terms, unpopular tax increases during the war, and a burden of debt at the end which was almost as large (at 2,350 million *livres*) as that left by Louis XIV (2,600 million) at the end of his reign. The impact on royal finances can be measured by the proportion of the government's revenue which went on servicing its debt — 30 per cent before the Seven Years War, 60 per cent after it. The debt incurred during this war indicates that long before the War of American Independence the Old Regime's foreign policy and its financial structures had become dangerously incompatible.

Economies in royal expenditure, which was now largely devoted to war, preparations for war, servicing war debts, and paying for the court of Versailles, were politically impossible. Accordingly, a long succession of talented and resourceful finance ministers struggled to increase revenue, cover deficits, and liquidate debts. Some also tried to improve the efficiency of tax collection and promote economic growth, and in the last two decades of the Old Regime, several turned their attention to securing more effective control over the disbursement of revenue. But the main preoccupation was always to maximize income.

d) Raising taxes

To understand the magnitude of the problem facing the ministers, it is vital to remember that they did not enjoy that great boon of modern public finance, the ability to deduct tax from incomes at source. Income tax, as we understand it, became feasible only in the modern economy with its large concentrations of salaried and waged employees, from whose earnings the employer deducts tax on behalf of the state. It is doubtful whether the large amounts of tax now levied in this way would be tolerated if the taxpayer had physically to hand over the sum demanded in cash, instead of merely being informed on a pay slip that it has already been deducted. Direct taxation was difficult to levy in pre-industrial Europe, not just in France but even in Britain and the Dutch Republic, because taxpayers usually had to hand over the sums required of them in cash.

Another reason for resistance to taxation lay in its arbitrary relationship to the ability to pay. Accurate assessment of income was impossible. The vast majority of taxpayers in France were peasant small-holders, many of them subsistence farmers only marginally involved in the money economy. Even keeping a record of the extent and value of the land they worked was beyond the capacity of the Crown's fiscal administration. So the starting point for the *taille*, the main direct tax levied on the peasants, was not what they could afford to pay but how much the Crown needed to raise. This sum was allocated among the localities in a rough-and-ready fashion, and the peasant community was left to assess and collect whatever proportion of the total charge each household had to pay. The bases of assessment were far from satisfactory. Land registers used in the south and south-west, *pays de taille réelle*, were rarely up to date because they were costly to revise. Sources of income other than land were ignored in these areas. Elsewhere, in the *pays de taille personnelle*, assessments were based on 'presumed wealth'. Such arrangements were plainly unsatisfactory for the Crown. Its main revenues were levied by the taxpayers themselves, who concealed their real wealth, delayed payment and grumbled incessantly to demonstrate that they were overtaxed.

Taxation depended in effect on consent, which was readily given only to taxes which were customary. New taxes and increases in old ones encountered resistance, and coercion often triggered rebellion. A steep increase in the amount of *taille* demanded (but not necessarily paid) in the first half of the seventeenth century, from about 15 million *livres* to about 55 million, resulted in endemic tax revolts from about 1630 to about 1660. The solution then adopted was to try to hold the amount of revenue raised by the *taille* steady, while boosting indirect taxes in compensation. This policy began to show results in the eighteenth century, especially after 1740, when the relative importance of the *taille* declined and the amount demanded fell relative to the increase in population and wealth.

Indirect taxes (that is, taxes on goods and trade) had much to recommend them as a source of revenue: their yield increased at a faster rate than that of direct taxes in the eighteenth century, and they had the additional advantage of bringing in large sums of ready money at regular intervals, because the Crown leased the right to collect them

to private entrepreneurs, the Farmers General, in return for fixed cash payments. But indirect taxes did nothing to allay popular hostility. They were socially regressive, most being levied on essentials — salt, tobacco and alcoholic beverages. This raised the cost of living, particularly for the urban lower classes. They were also arbitrary taxes, because tax rates on salt and alcohol varied from one part of France to another. Their real cost to the taxpayer, like that of the *taille*, may have been eroded by inflation during the eighteenth century (as P. Mathias and P. O'Brien claim), but this did not diminish the resentment they caused, especially among urban wage-earners whose income was also eroded by inflation. Hostility was mostly directed against the large bureaucracy employed by the Farmers General to collect these taxes, the vexatious procedures used, and the savage penalties inflicted on those who tried to evade them.
[DOCUMENT II]

Accordingly, the Crown's long-term strategy was to undermine the favoured treatment enjoyed by the privileged. These were not simply the clergy and nobles, but also certain provinces and towns which traditionally benefited from special tax deals negotiated with the government. Repeated efforts were made to establish universal liability on a uniform basis, by means of a succession of new direct taxes, starting with the *capitation* (1695), the *dixième* (1710) and, finally and politically most important, the *vingtième* (1749). The government did not find it at all easy to get the social élite, traditionally exempt from taxation, to pay these new taxes. The first two achieved little: the taxes themselves survived, but their original intention was subverted. Thanks to the influence which they exerted at court, the clergy were allowed to commute the *capitation, dixième*, and even the *vingtième*, into special payments raised by themselves, while nobles were assessed separately from commoners for the *capitation* and *vingtième*, and paid far less in proportion to their income. The *dixième* was, in any case, an 'extraordinary' tax, to be levied only in time of war and therefore intermittent — 1710–17, 1733–6, 1741–9.

Yet there is evidence that French governments were more successful than British both in levying direct taxation in the eighteenth century and in getting the social élite to pay its share. According to estimates by Mathias and O'Brien, direct taxes in France normally yielded almost half of total tax revenue in time of peace, and between 50 per cent and 60 per cent in wartime, which is two to three times greater than the proportion of total tax income produced by direct taxes in Britain. Their success in taxing the privileged is indicated by the fall in the importance of *taille*. It accounted for about half of direct tax revenue in 1725–6, but less than 30 per cent in the 1780s.

The *vingtième*, a 5 per cent tax on income, introduced in 1749 when the War of Austrian Succession was over, had no limit as to its duration and was clearly intended by Machault, who devised it, to be a permanent, regular source of revenue paid by all, privileged and non-privileged alike. The Church secured exemption in December 1751, but there were no other significant concessions until the outbreak of the Seven Years War. The government then agreed, in return for increases in the rate at which the *vingtième* was levied, that the declarations of income, on the basis of which individual tax liability was calculated, were no longer to be verified by the trained professional assessors appointed for this task. This meant that existing assessments would not be raised in line with increases in income. This was a significant concession at a time when the economy was buoyant, and wealth and inflation were rising. Terray was therefore prompt to take advantage of Maupeou's coup against the parlements and in November 1771 ordered the resumption of the work of checking tax declarations and adjusting assessments in line with income; he also increased the rate of tax from 5 per cent to 10 per cent. War again undermined the prospects of permanently establishing this tax as originally intended: the work of the *vingtième* assessors was again suspended in 1782 in return for a further 5 per cent increase in the tax rate. What this ding-dong battle over the *vingtième* indicates is the value both sides attached to it. Levied at 5 per cent it was worth 22–5 million *livres*; levied at 15 per cent (1760–3, 1782–6) it was worth about as much as the *taille*.

e) Credit and indebtedness

No matter how healthy its income, borrowing, then as now, was an essential component in the financial operations of government. Cash-flow was a general problem. All governments needed to take out short-term loans to cover the lag between the arrival of revenue, which dribbled in slowly and in small amounts, and its disbursement, which often required large cash expenditures at short notice. Long-term borrowing was needed to finance wars, which were never paid for out of current income. Extra taxes levied during wars were used to service the debt incurred. When popular resistance prevented government from adding to the tax burden, expedients such as forced loans, often called 'free gifts', would be demanded of corporate bodies such as parlementary magistrates, provincial estates and town councils, whose members were vulnerable to pressure because they had privileges to protect. These 'voluntary contributions' were surrendered reluctantly in dribs and drabs, so, like taxes, they would be used as collateral to secure loans from financiers. Batches of venal offices, which conferred noble status or tax exemption, were also treated as collateral for loans, which is why, when the market among individuals for such offices dried up, corporate groups, such as judges, tax officials and town councils, had to be bullied into buying them. Expedients such as these may appear bizarre, but, like taxes in Britain assessed on houses, windows, servants and carriage horses, they were a rational response to the circumstances in which finance ministers had to operate.

The problem with debt is not incurring it, but getting rid of it. The method traditionally favoured by the French monarchy was to cancel a large part of its debts at intervals. It did this by putting the financiers from whom it had borrowed money on trial, usually shortly after the end of a war, and inflicting heavy fines on them. This method of treating creditors damaged royal credit for a time and it could not be used if a resumption of hostilities was anticipated. But in the seventeenth and early eighteenth centuries it did not make the government unpopular because financiers were loathed by the public, which readily blamed them for the country's financial ills. By the latter part of the eighteenth century, however, financiers could no longer be used as scapegoats. They were respectable members of the affluent élite who married their daughters to the sons of aristocrats or to promising bureaucrats; they owned venal offices in the central financial administration; and they provided the Crown with short-term loans against the security of future tax yields. The Crown's short-term debt to these financial entrepreneurs, which according to Bosher greatly exceeded that owed in *rentes* (or government bonds) at the end of the Old Regime, gave them considerable influence over the outcome of its final crisis.

f) American independence and the pursuit of prestige

That final crisis was precipitated by the War of American Independence, which purely in terms of military success and international prestige was a good war, one that was popular in France. The Treaty of Versailles (1783) was the first major international peace settlement in the eighteenth century in which the French could take unqualified pride. The monarchy under Louis XVI appeared to have regained an ascendancy as peerless as that enjoyed by Louis XIV in the early years of his personal rule. But it proved to be a hollow, short-lived triumph, one which ushered in the Revolution. For that reason it is usually considered within the context of France's domestic financial history. But the war itself merits attention for the light it sheds on French foreign policy.

It demonstrates that France was not a prisoner of its geography. It vindicates Fleury's belief that France could concentrate its military effort overseas if it remained on the defensive in Europe. Vergennes, the foreign minister responsible for French intervention in North America and the strategy which ensured its success, achieved the isolation of Britain by respecting the neutrality of Hanover and the integrity of the southern Netherlands. It was more easily accomplished than in 1740 because the two German powers were preoccupied with eastern Europe and Britain was on bad terms with the Dutch; but the essential condition for its success was French willingness to rely on its strong defensive position on the Continent and to recognize that territorial expansion was not feasible. This was the assumption behind the impressive expansion of the French navy, a policy pursued consistently by a succession of ministers, starting with Choiseul after the Seven Years War, and one for which funds were not stinted. France entered the war in 1778 with a large modern fleet which, combined with that of Spain and later the Dutch, denied Britain naval superiority and led to the surrender at Yorktown.

The flaw in this strategy lay in its objective. French policy after the humiliation of the Seven Years War was dedicated not to the pursuit of tangible gains, as it had been under Fleury, but simply to securing revenge against Britain. French self-esteem had been badly hurt by repeated defeats in the course of a long rivalry, which stretched back to Louis XIV's reign and was likened by contemporaries to that of classical times between Rome and Carthage. It followed that Britain, the modern Carthage, had to be humbled. Only then would France's international prestige be restored and its ascendancy in Europe assured. The recovery of its former status was not allied to any material goal. Intervention in the American war was not prompted by hopes of regaining territory lost in the Seven Years War. Indeed, even the occasion for the resumption of hostilities was fortuitous. It might well have happened earlier, in 1770, as a result of the dispute between

Britain and Spain over the Falkland Islands, had it not been for the economic and financial crisis in France at that time. Preoccupation with status was obviously inherited from Louis XIV, but status was only one of Louis XIV's aims, and was achieved by pursuing tangible objectives, such as the acquisition of territory to strengthen France's frontiers. Those who came after Louis seem to have had difficulty reorientating foreign policy once the frontiers had been secured and, with the exception of Fleury, they allowed foreign policy to become entirely dominated by the pursuit of intangibles, such as reputation and ascendancy, with disastrous consequences.

Louis XVI himself, to do him justice, was far from enthusiastic about giving aid to rebels against a fellow monarch. Turgot and Necker were also opposed to French intervention in the war, knowing that it would ruin their efforts to rehabilitate the monarchy's finances. But Turgot was dismissed in 1776, and Necker had negligible influence on over-all policy. Their fears were entirely justified: the war cost over one billion *livres*, according to the best modern estimate (that is, average annual expenditure was about the same as it had been during the Seven Years War), but contemporaries were not aware of this burden because of the way it was financed. Necker managed to raise loans to fund the war effort without increasing taxes, an achievement which ensured popularity in his lifetime but which, until recently, led him to be dismissed by most historians as a charlatan. [DOCUMENT III]

g) Necker and his legacy

The traditional view is that Necker financed the American war by borrowing at exorbitant rates of interest in order to avoid unpopular and politically dangerous increases in taxation, and in so doing built up a huge public debt. A further charge against him is that just before leaving office in 1781 he published a set of accounts, the notorious *Compte rendu*, which were inaccurate and deliberately misled both the king and the country as to the true state of royal finances. This created an unjustified sense of confidence, which made it difficult for his successors to impose new taxes or carry out essential reforms. His financial maladministration was thus assumed to have been directly responsible for the crisis of 1787–8 which precipitated the Revolution.

This damning verdict has been challenged by Bosher, whose study of the way in which royal finances were administered, combined with research into Necker's loans by Harris, sheds a much more favourable light on his ministry. It is now understood that wars were always funded by borrowing, and that Necker was acclaimed by his contemporaries not because he raised loans to pay for the American war, but because he managed to service them out of ordinary revenue. He avoided the need for additional taxation by running the royal financial machine more efficiently and economically. His reforms included removing some of the indirect taxes from the charge of the Farmers General and arranging for them to be levied by government officials, at the same time abolishing a substantial number of the most senior venal offices in the central financial administration. In this way he reduced the costs of running this machine and improved his control over it, his main aim being to rescue the financial administration from the clutches of the financiers and place it under the effective supervision of the Crown. [**DOCUMENT IV**]

The case for Necker is powerful, but not without its weaknesses. Some of the loans he raised, specifically the life annuities, *rentes viagères*, bearing interest at 10 per cent, are open to criticism and were criticized by contemporaries. Harris argues that they had less impact on royal finances than Necker's opponents claimed, but the scandal caused, especially when it became known that some had been taken out by Swiss bankers in the name of young girls of Geneva whose life expectancy was more than fifty years, did considerable damage to Necker's reputation and that of the government. An even more fundamental objection is that the success of Necker's borrowing policy depended on the maintenance of his reforms and economies, which in turn depended on Necker remaining in office for a long period, and this was very unlikely. A rapid turnover of ministers had been one of the chief characteristics of French government since the death of Fleury in 1743, and the rate was particularly high among those in charge of finance. Necker had no reason to assume that his tenure of office would break this pattern; on the contrary, his position was weak from the start, and his reforms provoked a storm of opposition among some of the most powerful vested interests in France. This makes it difficult to accept Harris's basic defence, that Necker, in his financing of the American war, was simply doing what was done in Britain. There the National Debt was indeed huge, and servicing it took 50 per cent of government revenue, but public confidence and the continuity on which it depended were assured by the British Parliament. The court of Versailles, with its factionalism and intrigue, provided no such stability.

The fall of Necker had the worst possible consequences for royal financial policy. His successors continued to raise loans, and in fact borrowed more than he did. During the period 1776–81, Necker raised 530 million *livres*; Joly de Fleury in 1781–3 raised 252 millions; Calonne in 1783–7 raised 653 millions. While they maintained his improvements in the levying of indirect taxes, they undid his major achievement, the purge of financiers from the central financial administration. Joly de Fleury introduced tax increases, but in return for raising the *vingtième* from 10 per cent to 15 per cent, he had to halt the verification of declarations of income. Necker, in the mean time, was not idle: in 1784 he published a three-volume study, *On the Administration of Finances in France*, which explained precisely what was wrong with the financial administration and how its shortcomings could be cured. The stage was set for the Assembly of Notables.

3. The Crown, the Parlements and the Church

The incompetence of the French performance in the wars of the mid eighteenth century was underscored by a succession of defeats for the government at home. The Parlement of Paris took advantage of the Seven Years War and the Crown's need for tax increases to force it to abandon its prolonged campaign to eradicate the religious reform movement known as Jansenism. This was shortly followed by an unprecedented alliance among all the parlements, which drove the king to order the dissolution of the Society of Jesus, long the object of Jansenist denigration. These successes encouraged the parlements to adopt a far tougher attitude to the government's fiscal policy than they had done previously, and by the end of the Seven Years War their political authority appeared almost to outweigh the Crown's.

a) The thorn of Jansenism

The Parlement of Paris was presented with the opportunity to assert itself by Christophe de Beaumont, Archbishop of Paris, who was determined to put an end once and for all to the Jansenist tendency in French Catholicism. He and a few like-minded bishops regarded the Jansenists as heretics and sought either to force them to conform or to exclude them from the Church. The archbishop's campaign was the climax to a century-long struggle against these Catholic dissidents, and, like all earlier efforts at their suppression, had the effect of conferring the halo of martyrdom on the victims and of exacerbating the problems it was designed to resolve.

The Jansenists have generally evoked sympathy from historians. They were a small minority who withstood decades of persecution by both Church and state. In doing so, they upheld central principles of western philosophical tradition: that conscience is the ultimate court of appeal in matters of belief; and that reason decides matters of fact. They also resisted the influence of the Jesuits, a religious order often regarded with suspicion both inside and outside the Catholic Church. Pascal, a leading Jansenist, scientist and writer on religion, scored a notable success against them in the seventeenth century by exposing to public ridicule what Jansenists believed to be the Jesuits' all-too-accommodating penitential ethic. Yet there was an unattractive side to the Jansenists. Their capacity for sustained righteous indignation and wilful contentiousness was seldom moderated by self-doubt. They were 'the awkward squad' *par excellence* and, given their record, it is hardly surprising that they came under attack from ecclesiastical and secular authorities alike.

The Jansenists believed that their version of Christianity, whose emphasis on predestination and efficacious grace was similar to Calvinism, was the only true faith. They continued to defend Jansen's book on St Augustine's theology even after it had been condemned by the papacy. They attacked Richelieu's foreign policy and associated with those who opposed Mazarin in the Fronde. These stands were courageous, and provocative, at a time when open opposition to the teaching of the Church was deemed heresy and opposition to the authority of the state treason. In the eighteenth century they took up the cudgels on behalf of Gallicanism (when it was losing ground to ultramontanism in both royal and episcopal circles in France) and challenged the traditional hierarchical structure of the Church, demanding a much enhanced role for the lower clergy, and even for the laity, in its governance. Above all they relentlessly drew attention to the shortcomings of the papal bull, *Unigenitus*, promulgated in 1713, even to the extent of appealing against it to a General Council of the Church.

Unigenitus was indeed a source of embarrassment, even to Louis XIV. But since he had sought it, he was obliged to do all he could to get it accepted by the French Church. Its shortcomings have been eloquently analysed by John McManners. It condemned 101 propositions in a book by a leading Jansenist, Quesnel, *Moral Reflections on the New Testament*. This was a popular work of piety, first published as far back as 1668, which had gone through several editions and been recommended by many eminent clergy, including the Pope who later condemned it. The text of the bull was defective in form since it pronounced a general anathema on all the 101 propositions without specifying the precise degree of error of each. It was also dubious in substance. Though some of the condemned propositions were indeed heretical, others were perfectly orthodox, and some were actually extracts from the New Testament. Little wonder that the French bishops were reluctant to accede to pressure from Louis XIV to endorse the bull, and they refused to give it their unanimous or unqualified approval. The Parlement of Paris was also alarmed by *Unigenitus* because (according to its reading of the text) it apparently violated one of the chief tenets of Gallicanism: that the king was not subject to ecclesiastical authority in temporal matters. During the first decades of his personal rule, Louis XIV's championship of the independence of the French Church had been as ardent as the most committed Gallican could wish. But there had been a change of course in the 1690s which disquieted the Parlement, and *Unigenitus* seemed to confirm their fears. Instead of submitting to the king's wishes, as they had done for most of his personal rule, they refused to register the bull of their own volition and Louis had to impose it on them by *lit de justice*.

Matters were made infinitely worse when over 3,000 French clergy appealed against the bull to a General Council of the Church. Clement VIII responded to this challenge to his authority in 1718 by threatening the appellants with excommunication. This made the dispute a fight to the finish and explains the failure of the Regent Orleans's attempt to plaster over the split in the French Church. Fleury sought to end it by depriving appellant clergy of their benefices, but he also tried to minimize public agitation by dissuading the bishops from unnecessary zeal. His motive seems to have been to restore order and unity among the clergy, rather than to enforce *Unigenitus* as a rule of faith. He was therefore against denying its opponents the sacraments.

b) *Refusal of sacraments and the* Grandes Remontrances

No such reservations inhibited Christophe de Beaumont. Soon after he became Archbishop of Paris in 1747, he ordered parish *curés* within his jurisdiction to refuse the sacraments to incorrigible opponents of *Unigenitus*. Those suspected of being in this category were to be required to produce a certificate of confession signed by a priest who accepted the bull and could therefore be relied on to ascertain whether penitents did so too. These tactics, which led to men and women of irreproachable character being denied the sacraments even as they lay dying, caused public scandal and provoked a major political crisis when the victims of this harassment sought redress from the Parlement of Paris. They did so by invoking a long-standing right which entitled French Catholics to appeal to the secular courts against alleged abuses of ecclesiastical authority. The measured pace of judicial proceedings was ill-adapted to deal with appeals against spiritual sanctions by or on behalf of the dying, so when Louis XV asked the Parlement to refer all such appeals immediately to him, at first it complied. The king dealt with them tactfully by assigning an amenable priest to succour the dying. But the judges were uneasy about the regular use of the royal prerogative to decide legal cases, especially since the *curés* who had refused extreme unction continued to do so with impunity.

It was the repeated refusal of sacraments by Bouëtin, *curé* of Saint-Etienne-du-Mont in Paris, which caused the Parlement to start hearing appeals itself. The result was a long and angry confrontation between Crown and Parlement, in which both sides took extreme positions. The Parlement responded to appeals in a much more abrasive way than the king, ordering priests to administer sacraments to Jansenists, arresting and imprisoning them when they resisted, and declaring that *Unigenitus* was not an article of faith. Thus, the Parlement acted as if it had authority over matters that were intrinsically spiritual. The king tried to halt this provocation by transferring cases concerning the refusal of sacraments from the Parlement to the royal council. But the Parlement refused to recognize the decisions of the royal council in such cases and protested to the king in remonstrances which became increasingly vehement in tone and radical in content. In February 1753 Louis ordered the suspension *sine die* of all legal proceedings arising out of refusal of sacraments. The Parlement was outraged that the king should thus set aside the legal rights of his subjects and spent two months drawing up the longest and most famous remonstrances it ever issued. These were the *Grandes Remontrances* of 9 April 1753, which the king decided not to receive. He had requested and been given a résumé of the matters to be covered in them and did not like what he saw. His rejection of these remonstrances was yet another abrogation of fundamental rights in the eyes of the Parlement, which reacted by suspending all judicial hearings. The king retaliated by ordering all the magistrates into exile. They hit back by publishing the remonstrances he had rejected.

Louis's apprehension that they would be inflammatory was entirely fulfilled. The act of publication was in itself subversive. Remonstrances had hitherto been confidential submissions to the king. The publication of the *Grandes Remontrances* converted them into a political manifesto, an appeal to the general public. They presented three main arguments. One was strongly anticlerical, insisting that from time immemorial the Church had been engaged in a never-ending struggle to dominate the state, and was in danger of (at last) succeeding because Louis was less resolute than his forebears in defence of the state against clerical encroachment. Another theme was the inviolability of the law, the very foundation of the state. To flout the law as the king had done when he denied his subjects their right to appeal against refusal of sacraments was to undermine the monarchy itself. Neither of these arguments was original, though they were developed with rare vehemence. What was new to parlementary propaganda was the claim that the state was founded on a contract between king and people. This was given great prominence at the beginning of the remonstrances, and is cleverly presented in the form of quotations from such unimpeachable authorities as Bossuet and Louis XIV. [DOCUMENT V]

This manifesto was confident and uncompromising in tone. Its subversive argument made its success as a publication all the more damaging to the Crown. Yet the government had to give way. The Parlement won this particular round in the quarrel because the sub-stitute court set up to replace it, the *Chambre Royale*, was boycotted by lawyers and litigants, thereby causing havoc in the administration of justice in about one-third of France. Since the *parlementaires* were irremovable, it was the government which had to climb down.

The government's surrender to the judges was almost total. They were recalled from exile, and their stance on the question of the refusal of sacraments was endorsed in a royal declaration of September 1754, known as the Declaration of Silence. This was intended to put an end to the affair by imposing a ban on all mention of *Unigenitus*, but it was not acceptable to the relentless archbishop. Christophe de Beaumont instructed parish priests to continue as before, even though they could be prosecuted by the Parlement if they complied. The predicament of *curés* who were unfortunate enough to have moribund Jansenists among their parishioners was unenviable. They faced interdiction if they disobeyed the archbishop and deport-ation if they defied the Parlement. All clergy were now confronted by hostility from the general public. Its anger towards sacrament-refusing priests rapidly developed into an indiscriminate and open anticlericalism, and a growing disinclination to attend church services.

c) The failure of compromise

Nor did the restoration of the Parlement lead to improved relations with the Crown. At least some members of the royal council were intent on clipping the wings of the judges, and the result was an escalation of the conflict in 1755 and 1756, when the royal council found against the Parlement in two jurisdictional disputes. At least one decision was wrong in law, and both were impolitic, given the likelihood of war with Britain over the disputes between French and British settlers in North America.

The outbreak of war in 1756 made pacification at home urgent. A split in the General Assembly of French Clergy on the question of *Unigenitus* facilitated an approach to Rome for guidance, and Benedict XIV was prepared to be accommodating. His encyclical of October 1756 deliberately avoided describing the bull as a rule of faith, and paved the way for the royal declaration of December 1756. This permitted priests to refuse the sacraments to those whose opposition to *Unigenitus* was flagrant; but since the bull was not a rule of faith, they were forbidden to question penitents about their attitude to it. The right of ecclesiastical courts to deal with cases concerning sacraments was affirmed; but appeal to the secular courts was permitted if such cases involved public scandal. At the same time, the parlements were forbidden to order priests to administer the sacraments. These terms were sane and balanced but, like many compromises, they antagonized both sides to the dispute. The Archbishop of Paris and other members of the ecclesiastical hierarchy had staked too much on enforcing *Unigenitus* as a rule of faith to abandon it without protest, even though the Pope made it clear in January 1757 that the king's declaration had his approval. The judges were resentful because the declaration denied them the right to require priests to administer the sacraments. What caused even more outrage was the imposition of disciplinary measures, designed to prevent them from ever again organizing the kind of opposition they had mounted during the *Unigenitus* dispute, and the suppression of two of the lower chambers in the Parlement, whose members were more militant than the rest.

The government expected resistance but not on the scale it encountered. The *lit de justice* of 13 December 1756, which imposed these measures, was followed by the resignation of most of the judges, including the more senior and conservative. The sixteen judges deemed to be the ringleaders were then ordered into exile. Once again the Parlement's ability to paralyse the administration of justice caused the government to give way. The Parlement was rehabilitated in September 1757, the attempt to curb the judges' political activity was abandoned, and the secular courts regained the right to institute criminal proceedings against *curés* who refused the sacraments in the name of *Unigenitus*. This was a sharp about-face on the part of the Crown, which did not intervene to protect the fifteen Paris *curés* who were prosecuted between 1758 and 1763 for refusal of sacraments and punished with deportation. Several bishops were induced to resign their sees. Christophe de Beaumont, who would not, was exiled to his family seat in Périgord.

d) Disasters of the Church

The French Church was the first victim of this sorry episode. *Unigenitus* and the attempt to enforce it left the clergy weakened by internal strife and in conflict with the state at a time when Christianity itself was being challenged by radical intellectuals. The bishops were divided over *Unigenitus*. Many who accepted it did so in a spirit of compliance, not conviction, and were unenthusiastic about trying to impose it as an article of faith. Bishops who were zealous supporters of the bull alienated the lower clergy, making them receptive to ideas that were subversive of existing ecclesiastical structures. Jansenist priests at first adopted Gallicanism to justify their resistance to *Unigenitus*. They adopted the traditional Gallican position: definitions of doctrine by the Pope were authentic only if they enjoyed universal assent; if they were controversial, a general council was the ultimate authority; in its absence French bishops could pronounce on papal bulls. But the way in which most French bishops succumbed to pressure to accept *Unigenitus* undermined respect for the episcopacy as a defence against Rome. The persecution of appellants, combined with other causes of resentment, some of long standing (like the maldistribution of ecclesiastical wealth) and others more recent (like the increase in the bishops' powers over the parish clergy), led the Jansenists to look for an alternative source of authority for their stand.

They found it in ideas put forward by Edmond Richer in the early seventeenth century. Richerism stood for a kind of French Catholic presbyterianism. It claimed that just as bishops were the successors of the apostles, parish priests were the successors of Christ's seventy-two disciples. That is, they constituted an ecclesiastical order created independently of the bishops and therefore not subordinate to them. This doctrine became the basis for demanding a more democratically organized Church, one which would give the lower clergy an enhanced role in its government. Some Jansenists wanted to go even further, to include the laity as well as parish priests in the government of the Church, and these attributed ultimate authority to the assembly of all the faithful. Members of the ecclesiastical hierarchy were simply delegates (they argued) whose authority derived from the faithful and could by implication be revoked. Support from the Parlement also led Jansenists to endorse its claim that in temporal matters the French Church was independent of the papacy but subordinate to the state.

So as early as the mid eighteenth century, and largely as a result of the conflict over *Unigenitus*, much of the intellectual groundwork had already been laid for the disasters which befell the Church during the Revolution. The split between the bishops and the *curés*, manifested in the support given to the Third Estate in 1789 by the parish priests who dominated the First Estate, had its origins in the disputes over *Unigenitus* between a largely ultramontane hierarchy and a lower clergy more sympathetic to the Gallican-Jansenist position. The principles which informed the Civil Constitution of the Clergy of 1790, with its repudiation of papal authority, election of *curés* and bishops, and subordination of the Church to the state, can also be traced back to this crisis. Anticlericalism and growing indifference to religious observance, which were such marked features of popular culture after 1740, had very deep roots — in the widespread reaction against post-Trent Catholicism with its hostility to popular religious practices and its highly repressive sexual ethic. The expression of such anticlericalism, however, may well have been made easier by the battle within the Church over *Unigenitus* and the refusal of sacraments.

e) The Parlement's defiance

The monarchy suffered even more than the Church from the struggle over *Unigenitus*. For over forty years the Crown had tried to enforce a papal bull of questionable validity and had failed. The final outcome was a blow to its prestige, but what was even more damaging was the reputation for despotism it acquired during the conflict. The educated élite in France had recently been reminded by Montesquieu, in *De l'esprit des lois* (1748), of the difference between absolutism and despotism. In an absolute monarchy like that of France, sovereignty belonged to the king alone in the sense that he shared it with no other institution. But in exercising it, the king must respect divine law, natural law, and the fundamental laws of the kingdom. A despot, on the other hand, was subject to no such constraints. His will was the law and his subjects had no protection against abuse of authority. Louis XV's frequent violations of what the parlements regarded as the inviolable limits on royal authority led to accusations of despotism against the Crown, and by the 1760s the distinction between absolutism and despotism had become blurred.

The Parlement of Paris justified its defiance of the Crown in the 1750s on the traditional grounds that because it was the guardian of the fundamental laws, it had the right and obligation to protest when the Crown contravened them. [DOCUMENT VI, (a) and (c)] Montesquieu gave fresh lustre to this argument by identifying the parlements as the main surviving 'intermediary bodies' in France whose task was to act as a buffer and a link between the Crown and the nation. The Parlement of Paris's repertoire of constitutional arguments was also enriched and radicalized by its alliance with Jansenists. Le Paige, a Jansenist lawyer, argued in his very influential *Lettres historiques sur les fonctions essentielles du parlement*, published in 1752–3, that the Parlement was the lineal descendant of the ancient General Assemblies of the whole Frankish nation, which had had the right to approve or reject all of the laws of the Merovingian kings. The Parlement could therefore legitimately resist the king because it embodied these primitive assemblies and, by implication, represented the French nation. What Le Paige was putting forward was the concept of national sovereignty, though it was not presented in these terms. The Parlement of Paris adopted this argument in 1755 and it became part of its case for constitutional government down to 1788.

An even more potent, and in the long run more influential, Jansenist thesis was taken up after Maupeou's coup against the parlements. This derived from the claim that ecclesiastical authority belonged to the whole assembly of the faithful and was delegated to the hierarchy. Adapted to a secular context, this doctrine made the king a delegate, responsible not to God but to the nation, which entrusted the exercise of its sovereign authority to the king. The trust placed in the king was conditional, and in the absence of the Estates-General it was the Parlement which represented the nation and ensured that the trust was not abused.

f) The king's response: the Flagellation Speech

The constitutional debate in which the Parlement was engaged was
not conducted in private. It penetrated beyond the libraries, to the
salons and dining rooms of the educated élite and even to the popular
classes. The rivalry between Crown and Parlement was a matter of
common knowledge. The walls of the capital were plastered with
notices announcing the mutually contradictory judgements of the two
institutions in cases concerning refusal of sacraments. Opinion in
Paris was overwhelmingly on the side of the Jansenists and the Parlement. Pamphlets sympathetic to their cause and hostile to the government and beneficed clergy sold well. The Parlement was a major
source of employment, direct or indirect, in the capital: when the
government exiled the judges to the provinces, it hurt many more
than the judges, lawyers and litigants. Perhaps the best evidence of
the spread of subversive ideas is Damiens's physical assault on the
king in January 1757, a few days after Louis XV had imposed disciplinary curbs on the Parlement of Paris and provoked the judges into
resigning. The record of his interrogation, analysed by Dale Van Kley
in a fascinating study of the whole affair, suggests that Damiens had
acted under the influence of the rhetoric and arguments of the
Jansenist-Parlementary cause. He inflicted a superficial knife wound
on the king, and its harmlessness seems to have been intentional. This
was not a bid to assassinate Louis that failed, but an attempt to jolt
him into falling in line with the Parlement. Damiens's interrogators
concluded that he was a solitary fanatic, but he was certainly not alone
in feeling disaffected. In the wake of the 'assassination' attempt, about
one hundred people were arrested for derisive or seditious remarks,
including expressions of regret that Damiens had not finished off the
king.

Louis XV eventually reacted to the erosion of his authority by
affirming it to the Parlement of Paris on 3 March 1766 in a particularly
trenchant statement which came to be known as the Flagellation
Speech. It was a response to more than the particular incident that
provoked it: it reflected the exasperation induced by years of conciliating the Parlement. Its restoration in 1757 had been followed by
a decade during which involvement in war and the Crown's financial
difficulties had forced ministers to humour the judges. This had had
humiliating consequences for the Crown. It had been obliged to listen
to lectures on constitutional history, based on myths and claims that
were subversive of royal authority. [**DOCUMENT VI, (b)**] It had had

to acquiesce in the dissolution of the Society of Jesus, a long-standing ally of the Crown. And it had been forced to abandon its plan to resume the verification of *vingtième* declarations in 1763 and even to invite the parlements to submit proposals on the best way to reform royal taxes.

What finally prompted the Flagellation Speech was the growing unity of action among the parlements, which increasingly supported each other in their battles with the Crown. This capacity for concerted action was most effective in the 1760s during the parlements' campaigns against the Jesuits and increases in royal taxes. It was justified by another new constitutional claim, the *union des classes*, which appeared for the first time in remonstrances of the Parlement of Paris of 27 November 1755 and which asserted that the parlements were all branches of a single institution. This notion could not be tolerated by the Crown because it meant that a quarrel with one parlement would become a quarrel with all. Louis XV's speech was itself occasioned by remonstrances from the Parlement of Paris about disputes between the Crown and the Parlements of Pau and Rennes. Apart from the political harassment which could be mounted in the name of the *union des classes*, it reinforced the parlements' claim to represent the nation. Louis's response was to claim untrammelled sovereignty, free of all constitutional limits — 'legislative power, unqualified and undivided, belongs to me alone' — which went well beyond any assertion ever made by Louis XIV in defence of royal authority. That this was not an empty claim was demonstrated less than five years later when Maupeou abolished the Parlement of Paris. **[DOCUMENT VII]**

g) Lines are drawn

The coincidence of the climax of the dispute over *Unigenitus* with the Seven Years War resulted in the disintegration of the crucial compromise between Church and state and that between the Crown and corporate society which had been achieved during Louis XIV's personal rule. The stability of the Old Regime depended on maintaining an equilibrium between principles that were mutually exclusive if pushed to their logical conclusion: between absolutism and the rule of law, and between papal supremacy and the independence, even though it was only temporal, of the French Church. The old balance was upset not by the Church's attempt to crush Jansenism, or the state's attempt to increase its revenue, but by the fact that they both occurred simultaneously and that both were profoundly unpopular. A final show-down was delayed for two decades because the economy was buoyant in the middle decades of the eighteenth century and because Louis XV had the good sense to rule out Choiseul's plans for a war of revenge against Britain. But the issues on which the last battle of the Old Regime would be fought were identified in the mid century crisis, the lines were drawn and the accompanying rhetoric rehearsed. What made an open clash unavoidable was the combination of Maupeou's attack on the parlements, the monarchy's failure to carry through the reforms that its ministers believed to be essential, and France's participation in the American War.

The traditional view of Maupeou's attack on the parlements is that it was a determined attempt to crush their opposition to the Crown once and for all in order to remove obstacles to reform, especially financial reform. Cobban and other historians who viewed the parlements as the grave-diggers of the Old Regime assumed that if Maupeou's reform had been upheld, if he and Terray had not been dismissed and if the old parlements had not been restored by Louis XVI shortly after his accession in 1774, then the Revolution might well have been avoided. This interpretation assumes that the monarchy was the main progressive and far-sighted force in France, that the opposition of the parlements was largely responsible for thwarting reforms, and that their opposition was motivated by selfish, reactionary considerations. Much of this interpretation is questionable and has been challenged by William Doyle, whose conclusions have been qualified and supplemented by John Bosher. What we are left with is a crisis whose origins were financial but which belongs essentially to the history of the rise of opposition to the Old Regime.

It was precipitated by the Crown's long- and short-term financial problems. In the 1760s the government had considerable difficulty in raising sufficient revenue to cope with both the burden of debt left by the Seven Years War and the continuation of heavy expenditure on building up France's naval and military strength in readiness for a resumption of hostilities with Britain. Attempts to keep up a level of taxation in peacetime that was more appropriate to wartime provoked persistent opposition, especially from provincial parlements. The toughest battle centred on Brittany. The government was intent on improving the roads to its naval ports on the Atlantic seaboard, but the Bretons were determined not to succumb to the burden this would place on them. The struggle between Crown and province became a personal battle between the military governor, the duc d'Aiguillon, and the attorney-general of the Rennes Parlement, La Chalotais. It reached a climax in the Parlement of Paris in 1770, when d'Aiguillon was put on trial at his own request in order to put a stop to accusations that he had abused his authority as military governor in pursuing a vendetta against La Chalotais. Louis XV personally intervened to halt the trial in June because it had become an inquest on government policy. This 'Brittany Affair' worsened relations between Crown and Parlement and predisposed the king, exasperated by decades of opposition, to agree to harsh measures against the court.

The other reason for such measures was an immediate and acute financial crisis caused by poor harvests which afflicted most parts of France at different times between 1768 and 1773. High food prices as usual caused a slump in manufactures and trade and a rise in unemployment. Collecting taxes became even more difficult than usual and several leading venal office-holders in the central financial administration, who financed the government's short-term debt, went bankrupt. Fears about the government's financial solvency were heightened when international investors withdrew their funds.

To cope with this emergency, Terray in February 1770 effected what amounted to a partial bankruptcy in order to avert the even greater catastrophe of general bankruptcy. He converted short-term debt, which took the form of notes issued by financiers on the government's behalf in anticipation of the tax revenues of 1770, into long-term debt. This operation denied the financiers the payments due to them in 1770 but it kept the government afloat financially because it permitted fresh notes to be issued against the security of the 1770 tax revenues. The damage this did to the Crown's credit meant that Choiseul's belligerent foreign policy was no longer feasible, and this was clearly signalled when Louis XV refused to allow France to be dragged into a war over the Falkland Islands. This in turn made it possible to abandon Choiseul's policy of conciliating the parlements. Their opposition to tax increases and fiscal reform had to be removed in order to secure an improvement in royal revenues. Whether the total package of reforms which had been implemented by April 1771 was what Maupeou had in mind when he threw down the gauntlet to the Parlement of Paris in November 1770 is doubtful. The crisis began with an attempt to curb the Parlement's ability to cause trouble. When the Parlement resisted, it was replaced with a substitute court, as had happened on two previous occasions (1732 and 1753–4). What was different about 1771 was that the king did not weaken, and some reforms were introduced in the judicial system.

If the precise motivation behind the reforms is not clear, their consequences are. They made possible Terray's next batch of fiscal and financial measures. The most important of these prolonged the second *vingtième* tax, due to end in 1772, for a further ten years, and ordered declarations of income to be properly checked and revised. Given the parlements' record of determined resistance to more than one *vingtième* tax in peacetime, and their unwillingness to allow the declarations of income to be revised, Terray's reforms are inconceivable without Maupeou's emasculation of the courts and can be seen as their most important practical consequence. Terray also suppressed some venal offices in the central financial administration and got better terms from the Farmers General for the lease of indirect taxes.

The increase in taxes following the reform of the parlements substantiated their claim that effective constraints on royal authority were needed to protect the nation against ministerial despotism. But Maupeou's success also demonstrated that the parlements themselves were ineffectual as barriers against abuse of power. The dramatic events of 1771 accelerated the decline in popular and élite respect for absolute monarchy and stirred up an impassioned debate between Maupeou's critics and his relatively few supporters on the political and constitutional issues raised by the reform. Some of those who opposed the attack on the parlements, the 'patriots', argued that a written constitution was the only safeguard against authoritarianism and urged the summoning of the Estates-General.

Louis XVI sacked Maupeou and Terray and abandoned the reform of the parlements shortly after his accession in 1774. He was advised to do this in order that his reign might be seen to be a fresh start and to placate the 'patriot' opposition. Louis XVI's action enhanced his own popularity but the damage which Maupeou's coup had inflicted on the reputation of the monarchy was not undone. The restoration of the old parlements and judges did not obliterate the knowledge that their existence depended on royal sufferance. This is not to argue that the end of absolutism was thereafter inevitable. But in any future crisis similar to that of 1770, the Crown would be confronted by more determined opponents who would have their slogan and strategy to hand: summon the Estates-General.

4. The Failure of Reform

After the wars of the mid eighteenth century, a succession of reforming ministers introduced a variety of measures to remedy the ills of the state and the economy. Most of these can be said to have failed in that they were either abandoned within a very short time or so severely amended that their original purpose was nullified. The result was to unsettle the regime by casting doubt on the validity of the old order. Attempts at reform encouraged expectations of change that were disappointed or only partially satisfied; they also aroused the hostility of powerful vested interests which were threatened but not defeated by them. Edmund Burke was impressed by the Crown's

> earnest endeavour towards the prosperity and improvement of the country . . . it had long been employed, in some instances, wholly to remove, in many considerably to correct, the abusive practices and usages that had prevailed in the state. . .

But he criticized it for being

> open, with a censurable degree of facility, to all sorts of projects. . . Rather too much countenance was given to the spirit of innovation, which was soon turned against those who fostered it and ended in their ruin. It is but cold, and no very flattering justice to that monarchy, to say, that, for many years, it trespassed more by levity and want of judgement in several of its schemes, than from any defect in diligence or in public spirit.

A later conservative, Tocqueville, expressed a similar conclusion with more detachment and sympathy in his well-known aphorism that despotism is at its weakest when it tries to reform itself.

The imperative behind reform was the Crown's determination to retrieve France's international ascendancy after the humiliation of the Seven Years War. That France, with a population and territory about three times that of Britain, should have been so clearly outclassed by its rival jolted the government and made it more receptive to radical proposals than it might otherwise have been. Some of the reforms, for instance the overhaul of the army and navy and the introduction of the *vingtième* tax, were obvious, conventional responses to defeat; others were not. The influence of a new kind of intellectual, the economist or physiocrat, can be seen in the plan to encourage the modernization of agriculture by lifting controls from the grain trade, permitting enclosures and ending collective rights of grazing on stubble. Outsiders, men like the *parlementaire* Laverdy and the Swiss banker Necker, were allowed to introduce measures which reduced the powers of the intendants and reversed the historic trend towards an increasingly centralized administration. Laverdy in 1764–5 restored to towns the right to elect their own officers, a right of which they had been deprived for over a century, and allowed them a measure of financial autonomy. Necker set up provincial assemblies in Berry (1778) and Haute-Guyenne (1779), with the intention of extending them to other provinces if the experiment went well.

Those responsible for improving France's military capability, the most straightforward task, enjoyed most success. The navy was overhauled and expanded and built up to the point where it could challenge British naval supremacy in the American War. Kellerman equipped the army with the best light artillery in Europe and Lavoisier provided it with the best explosives; military schools were set up to improve the training of officers; and Ségur's reform in 1781 tried to ensure that military commissions went to those most likely to have a serious interest in a military career. Some of the reforms designed to put government finances on a sound footing — the *vingtième* tax and improvements in the collection of indirect taxes — helped to extend the life of the regime, but traditional expedients such as Terray's partial bankruptcy and the borrowing of Necker and Calonne were probably just as important.

Most of these efforts to transform the regime were thwarted, quickly abandoned, or had only partial success. Turgot's attempt to abolish the guilds in 1776 failed. Plans to abolish internal customs barriers and to standardize weights and measures were shelved; hopes of creating a more competitive national market were consequently dashed. The new dispensation that Laverdy introduced in the towns was terminated in 1771, only six years after its introduction, and no attempt was made to generalize Necker's provincial assemblies until the eve of the Revolution, so France's over-centralized, overly-bureaucratic administration continued untouched. The *vingtième* tax as originally envisaged was sabotaged by the clergy, parlements and *pays d'états*, so it did not contribute as much as it ought to have done to royal finances. Many of the most significant measures brought in by Necker were undone when he fell from power, so the central financial administration remained expensive, poorly co-ordinated and in the grip of the financiers. The reform of the judicial system effected by Maupeou in 1771 was undone in 1774, and a similar attempt by Lamoignon in 1788 was abandoned within weeks: the old judicial hierarchy continued intact and the courts were as inaccessible, dilatory and expensive as ever. Controls on the grain trade were lifted in 1763–4, restored in 1770, lifted again, partially, in 1774, completely removed in 1787, and restored again in 1788, one of the worst instances of a 'stop-go' policy on record, which benefited neither producers nor consumers, and perhaps not even the middlemen.

a) Why did the reforms fail?

Responsibility for the failure of these reforms has traditionally been laid at the door of the vested interests threatened by them — courtiers, financiers, clergy, and especially the parlements. That the parlements have traditionally attracted most opprobrium from historians is understandable. Their opposition was the most public and, in the light of the notorious decree of September 1788, could readily be interpreted as having been inspired all along by selfish, reactionary motives. But it is no longer possible to see them, as Cobban did, as the villains of the piece, obstructing an enlightened monarchy which had the true measure of the country's needs. The judges' actions undoubtedly took account of their personal interests, but they were also influenced by public opinion, and above all by their determination to uphold the rule of law. This last was an end in itself for men of their profession, and the only formal defence against unbridled authoritarianism in a regime where political accountability was lacking. The effectiveness of the opposition which the parlements themselves could erect against the Crown must not be exaggerated: remonstrances and judicial strikes could be overcome with *lettres de jussion, lits de justice* and *lettres de cachet*. It was only when there was vacillation and division within the royal council and when public opinion was on the parlements' side, that is to say when their decisions were perceived to represent more than their professional or personal interests, that the judges could successfully defy the Crown. Maupeou's coup showed how easily a purposeful, united government could crush the parlements even when they enjoyed popular support.

Other opponents of reform were far less easily dealt with. The financiers, threatened by the efforts of Terray, Turgot and Necker to give the Controller-General authority over royal finances in fact as well as in name, were so well entrenched by the 1780s that in financial crises, like that of 1787–8, those who did not go under could hold the government to ransom. The Church had considerable influence over His Most Christian Majesty, even when the king was not particularly devout, and used it to preserve the tax privileges of the clergy and to delay the relaxation of the disabilities endured by Protestants and Jews. Courtiers were even better placed than prelates to influence the king, especially over the appointment of ministers, and took a particular interest in the person and policies of the Controller-General. They helped to bring down Turgot who made no attempt to cultivate a following among them — a foolish mistake, because the court was the natural constituency of ministers — and even cut expenditure on the royal household. Calonne's determination not to suffer the same fate partly explains why he was so profligate. Courtiers and court factions would not have enjoyed this influence if Louis XV and Louis XVI had been able to dominate the court as Louis XIV had done. But they could not. Even intendants, the key agents of the government in the provinces, could be very effective at impeding reforms which threatened their authority, as did all measures to achieve administrative decentralization. In one area, Burgundy, the obstruction of the local intendant, in alliance with the provincial estates, was so dogged that Laverdy's municipal reform was never implemented in that province. [**DOCUMENT VIII**]

Studies of reform measures and ministers suggest that the main reason for their failure is to be found in the inner workings of government itself. Historians like Bosher, Dakin, Doyle, Harris and Kaplan conjure up a depressing spectacle of irresolute kings and of discord among ministers whose bitter personal rivalries added to their differences over policies. The number and variety of reforms initiated and the succession of reforming ministers may suggest a reform 'campaign' or 'movement', but to use either of these terms would be misleading. There were reforms, there were ministers committed to reform, but there was no programme. Reforms were introduced fitfully, on what appears to have been a trial-and-error basis. Expediency, not policy, was their most common quality. There was no agenda which commanded general consent, no agreement as to priorities. No attempt was made to introduce the reforms in sequence so as to enhance the chances of overcoming opposition by dealing with it piecemeal. Talleyrand described the proposals put to the Assembly of Notables as more or less the result of what good minds had been thinking about for several years, which is true, but before 1787–8 that thinking had not been put together in a coherent package. The ministers associated with reform, Machault, Laverdy, Maupeou, Turgot, Necker and Calonne, differed about what was necessary and whether it was feasible. For Machault the priority was taxation; for Laverdy, liberalizing the grain trade and municipal self-government; for Maupeou, emasculating the Parlement of Paris and judicial reform; for Turgot, liberal economic reform; for Necker, getting a grip on the central financial administration; for Calonne, tax reform and a liberal economic policy.

Not only was there no consensus on policies and priorities, but the reformers were rivals for office and were prepared to denigrate and undermine each other to get it. Ministerial instability, one of the chief features of French government after the death of Fleury, obviously hampered reform: those who were responsible for financial and economic policy in the last decades of the Old Regime could achieve little because their tenure of office was so insecure and brief. [DOCUMENT IX] The contrast with Richelieu, Mazarin, Colbert, and Fleury is marked. Ultimate responsibility rests with France's kings. Louis XV appointed men of incompatible temperament and policies to the royal council, imagining that this would enable him to divide and rule. But he was too easily bored, too indecisive and indolent, to sustain the effort required by this tactic. Government became the plaything of court factions. Innovating ministers like Machault had to do battle with conservative rivals like d'Argenson, and the rate of attrition was severe, except for a brief period when Choiseul dominated the government. Louis XVI, like his grand-father, failed to give his ministers the consistent, intelligent backing needed for long-term success. His chief political adviser in the early years of his reign (1774–81), Maurepas, who was determined to make himself permanent and indispensable, was allowed to intrigue against any minister who appeared to be acquiring ascendancy over the king. Turgot was his first victim, but Maurepas would probably not have succeeded in ousting him without the help of Necker, who hoped to replace Turgot. Necker was similarly removed in 1781 by Maurepas conspiring with Calonne. Necker and Calonne engaged in bitter public recriminations in 1787, after the opening of the Assembly of Notables, as to which of them was the more responsible for the financial crisis. Loménie de Brienne led the attack on Calonne in the Assembly, replaced him when he was dismissed by the king, which was to be expected, but nevertheless took over Calonne's programme (which would be surprising in a system dominated by a parliament rather than a court). Calonne got his revenge a year later when, with the help of the king's younger brother, Artois, he effected Brienne's dismissal. Even Maupeou and Terray constantly intrigued against each other: they remained in office together, not because of any strong bond between them but because, though they were opposed by every court faction, they were supported by Mme du Barry.

These constant rivalries were not prompted solely by competition for office. There were genuine disagreements about the wisdom of particular policies, the most vexed and important after finance being liberal economic reform. Laverdy and Turgot were firmly committed to free trade and optimistic about its beneficial long-term effects. Terray, Turgot's immediate predecessor, was hostile to both political and economic liberalism. Necker seems to have accepted reluctantly that there was no alternative to free trade, but was pessimistic about market forces ensuring prosperity for all, and he insisted that the government must have the right to suspend free trade in grain when the harvest failed. Behind such policy differences lay a serious debate about economic liberalism among intellectuals, and to some extent their differences, like those of the ministers, reflect a conflict between generations. The promise of free trade seemed brighter in the prosperous 1750s and early 1760s than in the 1770s and 1780s, years of depression and chronic harvest shortfall.

The other key area of controversy was financial reform. Since the seventeenth century, governments had been chipping away at the fiscal privileges of the élite. Necker was sceptical about this, on the grounds that to impose equal liability to taxation on the nobility would increase revenue by twelve million *livres*, a mere 2 per cent. Necker's policy was to secure much tighter government control over the administration of revenue and expenditure and to make it more efficient by eliminating a large number of venal officials from the central government departments. These men were independent and difficult to discipline, not simply because they owned their posts and could not be dismissed but also because many of them were financiers involved in lending money to the government. Terray and Turgot had also favoured curbing their hold on government finances. Calonne, who had exactly the opposite viewpoint, perhaps because he had married the daughter of a financier, reversed Necker's reforms, restored the financiers to their offices, and returned to the traditional policy of eroding the tax privileges of the nobility and other favoured groups.

Fluctuations in royal policy were also the result of external opposition, actual or anticipated. Ministers could hardly help being affected by their awareness of the parlements' potential for trouble-making. The decade of relative peace between the Crown and the Parlement of Paris from the mid 1770s to the mid 1780s was not just because the Parlement had been cowed by defeat in 1771, but also because the government took good care not to antagonize it. There were no tax reforms, notwithstanding French entry into the American war, because Necker decided to service the debt incurred during the war by means of economies in the financial administration. When Calonne decided that major tax reform was unavoidable, he did not assume that because the Parlement had given no serious trouble for a decade it was therefore a broken reed. He persuaded an unenthusiastic Louis XVI to summon the Assembly of Notables in 1786 precisely because he hoped that its approval would enable him to overcome the anticipated opposition of the Parlement to reform.

Social unrest also weakened commitment to reform. Most of the changes were attempted during a period of persistent economic *malaise*, the result of agricultural depression combined with intermittent harvest failure, a combination which reduced demand for manufactures and increased unemployment. Liberal economic policy had little chance of succeeding in these circumstances. The lifting of controls on the grain trade in the 1760s occurred when a long period of mainly good harvests gave way to poor harvests. Dearth and high prices were popularly attributed to a government-inspired conspiracy, the *pacte de famine*, and aroused violent agitation for price-fixing and controls on distribution to protect the consumer. The police, among the most vociferous critics of an unregulated grain trade, made no very strenuous efforts to quell unrest because it justified their claim that they could not be expected to maintain order if they did not have the traditional regulations at their disposal. Laverdy's municipal reform was far from unpopular, but freedom of elections led to the divisions and excitements attendant on political contests. This was invigorating for those taking part, but alarming to a regime that was always anxious about social order and tended to magnify threats to it. The reform was repealed for mainly financial reasons, but the disturbance associated with elections provided its enemies with a powerful argument to justify its abandonment.

b) Absolutism and representation

This fear of unrest probably goes some way to explain the government's reluctance to grasp the nettle of representation. There was a strong body of opinion in the eighteenth century, both inside and outside government circles, in favour of involving local notables in public administration. After Laverdy's attempt to revive municipal administration had been abandoned, hopes were pinned on provincial assemblies as a means of bridging the gulf between the state and society. Turgot commissioned Dupont de Nemours to draw up plans for a nation-wide hierarchy of assemblies, at parish, district, and provincial level, the district and provincial assemblies being elected by and from the members of the assemblies immediately below. The possibility of crowning this edifice with a national assembly was also envisaged. Turgot had neither the time nor, perhaps, the conviction to implement this plan, but it inspired the similar proposal put by Calonne to the Assembly of Notables in 1787. Necker meanwhile had launched a pilot scheme of assemblies of a different kind in the provinces of Berry and Haute-Guyenne. But this remained an experiment, its chances of being extended prejudiced by the revelation that Necker intended these assemblies to take over the administrative and quasi-legislative functions of the parlements.

To go beyond the stages of plans and pilot schemes meant taking decisions on a number of vexed practical matters on which the role of the assemblies hinged. Were they simply to ease the burden on the intendants by taking over routine administrative tasks, such as tax collection and supervising public works, or were they to have some independent authority? Whom were they to represent — the traditional three orders or property-owners without distinction of legal status? Were they to be elected, and if so how? What was proposed or implemented by the government at various times suggests that the ministers concerned saw the assemblies facilitating the work of administration in the localities, including the introduction of reforms, but not initiating a gradual move to self-government. Their membership and activities were to be very largely under government control. There was no question of public elections to the assemblies, even on a restricted franchise, and the intendants had a veto over what they could do. On the other hand, those outside government circles who advocated provincial assemblies saw them both as a means of giving expression to popular sovereignty and as a check to government powers, especially those of the intendants. Turgot seems to have grasped that, even if assemblies were set up with purely administrative and consultative responsibilities, they might well become an independent political force that would not necessarily lend itself to the achievement of the government's objectives.

It was the government's unwillingness to contemplate even modest breaches of absolutism which ruined its chance of effecting change under its control. Revolutionary change became unavoidable because the Crown resisted pressure to share its hitherto unqualified political authority. Government ministers, especially during Louis XVI's reign, were intent on improving the economy, government finance, and the administration of justice even if they differed about the methods to be used. There was little inclination, except perhaps on the part of Necker, to share power with even that sector of society most likely to support their efforts, the property-owning élite. Louis XVI and his ministers have been described as liberal because they were working towards more rational and efficient institutions. They were also sensitive to public opinion, even to the extent of trying to influence and manipulate it. But such characteristics are not uncommonly found in authoritarian regimes. Liberalism, in the classic sense of government accountable to elected representative institutions, was not their aim; they were not prepared to concede power voluntarily. This became obvious during the Assembly of Notables.

c) The Assembly of Notables

The decision to summon an Assembly of Notables, a body which had last met in 1626–7, was itself evidence that reform could not be carried out by royal authority alone. The support of some independent body, which might be deemed to represent society, was required to overawe opposition from those who either had a vested interest in the status quo, or would demand an unacceptable quid pro quo in return for agreeing to change. When Calonne came to the conclusion, in the middle of 1786, that a programme of radical reforms was needed to avert the immediate threat of bankruptcy and provide a surer financial and economic foundation for the future, he asked Louis XVI to submit this programme to an Assembly of Notables in the first instance in the hope that its approval would deter obstruction by the parlements. The king eventually agreed, with some misgivings, to what turned out to be the overture to revolution.

Historians have always been critical of Calonne's want of

judgement in assuming that because the Assembly of Notables was
nominated by the king it would therefore be docile, when its membership, fixed by tradition, comprised the cream of the privileged
élite. Otherwise Calonne has had, until recently, a good press. There
was sympathy for him because he was assumed to have inherited a
'poisoned chalice' from his predecessors, notably Necker, whose
Compte rendu of 1781 gave a misleading impression that government
finances were in good order, thereby obscuring the need for reform
and ensuring a hostile reception for unpalatable remedial measures
when they were eventually put forward. There was respect for the
comprehensive nature of the programme which Calonne presented to
the Notables. It appeared to provide a solution for all major ills, and
its merit seemed to be confirmed by the fact that Loménie de Brienne,
who supplanted Calonne, took it over more or less intact. Responsibility for Calonne's failure has generally been attributed to the selfish
myopia of the Notables in refusing to endorse reforms which, if
implemented, might have saved people like themselves, the privileged
élite, as well as the monarchy from destruction in the Revolution.

This assessment of Calonne has been revised downwards as
Necker's reputation has been revised upwards. Not all critics have
been converted by Harris's defence of the *Compte rendu* of 1781, but
most now accept that Necker's reform of the central administration of
finance was well-judged and that the financial catastrophe which
confronted Calonne in 1786 was largely of his own making. He could
hardly claim to have been misled by the *Compte rendu* since his
analysis of it helped Maurepas to secure Necker's dismissal. He
borrowed very heavily for as long as he could, without the excuse of
financing a war effort, and spent very unwisely. The Notables were
inclined to blame Calonne's profligacy for the royal debt; their
mistrust of him was increased when at first he refused to justify his
demand for new taxes by providing evidence of the state of the
Crown's finances. Once convinced of the need for reform, they were
prepared to concede the desirability of many of Calonne's proposals,
but they insisted that new taxes must be approved by the Estates-
General and accompanied by financial accountability. Several
members were intent on securing Calonne's removal from office,
including the archbishops, who had considerable independent experience of financial administration. To circumvent the resistance of these
formidable opponents, Calonne made the fatal mistake of appealing
over the heads of the Notables to the general public. He published his
reform proposals with a polemical introduction, the *Avertissement*

(also published separately as a pamphlet), which argued that the Notables were obstructing reform by stubbornly defending the tax privileges of the élite. This provoked outrage among the Notables and embarrassed the king who, forced to choose between them and Calonne, chose the Notables.

Loménie de Brienne had led the opposition to Calonne. Appointed first minister, he modified the reform programme to meet some of the criticisms of the Notables: he included the creation of a central treasury, advocated by Necker. But he too encountered entrenched resistance when he refused to accommodate the demand for financial accountability. That the Notables should insist on this is hardly surprising, given the disastrous consequences of the fluctuations in financial policy during the previous years and the large sums of additional revenue the government sought. To have agreed to new taxes without obtaining safeguards against the maladministration that had prevailed in the past would have brought the Assembly into disrepute. What was demanded, an independent Council of Finances, was the minimum acceptable check on ministerial despotism. The Assembly's refusal to give way caused Brienne to disband it, which turned out to have been an unwise move from his point of view. The parlements proved to be both more conservative and more radical than the Assembly of Notables.

The Parlement of Paris, which registered edicts authorizing most of the reforms, insisted, like the Assembly of Notables, that new taxes required the consent of the Estates-General. It eventually secured an undertaking that the Crown would summon that body by 1792 at the latest, in return for registering edicts providing for new loans and the continuation of existing taxes. Brienne hoped that by 1792 a solution would have been found for the government's financial problems: an Estates-General that did not enjoy the power of the purse would pose little threat to absolutism and might even be dispensed with altogether. If, after all, it had to be summoned, the newly inaugurated provincial assemblies would then be well established and could be used as electoral colleges; so there was a fair chance that they would produce a body sympathetic to the government's interests. This strategy — to reschedule the government's debts, overhaul the financial administration, and summon the Estates-General, if at all, when the crisis was past — came to grief as a result of the mishandling of the royal session at the Parlement of Paris in November 1787, when Louis XVI and Lamoignon, the Keeper of the Seals, rattled by criticism and misjudging its seriousness, decided on the spur of the moment to convert the meeting into a *lit de justice* and impose the registration of edicts authorizing loans. The protests against this violation of established procedure were led by the Duke of Orleans and resulted in *lettres de cachet* being issued to exile him and arrest others. The incident gave rise to a national campaign of protest, the revolt of the nobility, which undermined the Crown's financial position and, in the long run, led to Loménie de Brienne's dismissal and his replacement by Necker in August 1788.

In the mean time, Brienne and Lamoignon adopted a bold new strategy which raised the political tension dramatically. Lamoignon embarked on a reform of the parlements in the coup of May 1788 that was designed, like that of Maupeou in 1771, to emasculate them politically and to improve the administration of justice. Opinion, already suspicious of the government's intentions, was inflamed by this move, and the benefits conferred on litigants by this reform were lost sight of in the fury aroused by what was widely seen as an act of despotism. The Parlement of Paris, which got wind of it in advance, launched a pre-emptive strike in the form of its declaration of April 1788. Brienne made a bid to rally the support of the Third Estate to the Crown, by advancing the convocation of the Estates-General to May 1789 and by calling for advice on how it should be constituted and elected. He adopted the tactic used the previous year by Calonne: just as his predecessor had appealed against the Assembly of Notables to the non-privileged, so Brienne appealed against the parlements and nobility to the Third Estate. There was some chance of success: the leaders of the Third Estate, the *bourgeoisie de robe*, had not given the protests of the nobility significant backing except in Dauphiné, and they stood to benefit from Lamoignon's judicial reforms. This was a high-risk policy and to bring it to a successful conclusion required determination and a gift for political leadership which neither the king nor his ministers possessed. It also required luck, which was denied by the harvest failure of 1788. Dearth, as always, diminished tax revenue and the financial crisis which resulted gave Brienne's many enemies the opportunity to bring about his downfall. He was succeeded by Necker, who tried to appease public opinion by restoring the parlements. This meant abandoning the strategy of rallying the *bourgeoisie de robe* to the Crown, because they were alienated by Necker's annulment of Lamoignon's judicial reforms. The liberal nobility lost no time in making a powerful bid to secure for themselves the backing of the Third Estate.

5. The Revolution Becomes Radical

a) The voting and the structure of the Estates-General

What followed the meeting of the Estates-General proved to be unlike anything that might have been anticipated by those who had pressed for it to be summoned. The collapse of absolutism did not result in the acquisition of power by the dominant social class. The downfall of the Old Regime had been precipitated by a 'Whiggish' élite of the affluent and the enlightened, whose representatives in the Assembly of Notables and the Parlement of Paris had refused to rescue the monarchy from the consequences of its financial mismanagement. That élite had reasonably assumed that absolutism would be quickly replaced by a liberal regime of the kind eventually established in the nineteenth century, in which a limited constitutional monarchy was dominated by wealthy landowners, businessmen, professional men, and public officials. The transition took a generation of revolutionary upheaval and its outcome was always in doubt.

Earlier events in French history had been referred to as 'revolutions'. The term was commonly used of sudden, unexpected changes in the established order, like Maupeou's coup against the parlements in 1771 or Loménie de Brienne's inauguration of provincial assemblies in 1787. The Revolution of 1789 was soon seen to be different. It was not the work of ministers or court factions, but of a people. It was not an episode, soon over and done with, but a continuing crisis in which the fate of France and of humanity as a whole was perceived to be at stake. Those who had pressed for the convocation of the Estates-General, whether inside or outside government circles, had clearly expected it to be the means of carrying out institutional reforms of no mean significance. But none had seen it as the birth of a brave new world.

The Marxist interpretation readily explained the radicalism of 1789 as the overthrow of the old feudal order by the revolutionary bourgeoisie. Revisionist historians, having discarded the view that the upper echelons of French society were dominated by two mortally opposed classes and having adopted instead the concept of a dominant social class, have had a much more difficult task explaining why that class failed to secure a firm hold on power in 1789 and why one of the features of 1789 and succeeding years was a struggle between the nobility and the bourgeoisie. There is an understandable reluctance on the part of most historians to ascribe large events to relatively minor causes, but the radicalism of 1789 appears to stem from the composition of the Estates-General and the methods used to elect it. It was the adoption of a system of representation that was in part antiquated and in part modern which split the affluent enlightened élite and made privilege the dominant political issue in the early months of 1789.

The date first set for the meeting of the Estates-General would have allowed plenty of time for the government to work out a representational system more in keeping with contemporary social realities. Had Brienne remained at the helm and had his original timetable been adhered to, the Estates-General might well have been composed of delegates from the provincial assemblies inaugurated in 1787. This would certainly have given political predominance to the dominant social class. But bringing forward the date of the Estates-General from 1792 to 1789 ruled out any measured consideration of who should be represented and how. There was little time to study the responses of corporate bodies to whom Brienne appealed for their views on representation, and attempts to get Necker to determine the bases on which the Estates-General was to be chosen failed. Necker was not confident of royal backing — he was aware of Louis XVI's antipathy towards him — and was perhaps for this reason unwilling to do anything which might jeopardize his popularity at large.

The passive role which Necker adopted in all except financial matters was a significant factor in the events which transformed the Estates-General from a solution to yet another — and even greater — problem. Necker was entirely the wrong person to be chief minister at this juncture. His presence in the government was essential to the solvency of the monarchy, but after his earlier experience as finance minister he had been unwilling to settle for that office alone. However, the crucial problem facing the monarchy in 1788–9 was its political, not its financial, future and this Necker left to the Estates-General. He assumed that it would be well-intentioned and loyal to the Crown and that he would be able to conciliate any differences that arose in it.

Nor was the king capable of taking a decisive lead. Louis XVI, conscientious, anxious to do what was best for his people, was far from being the dolt he was made out to be by malicious court gossip. But having inherited what he took to be absolute authority, he was completely lacking in the practical attitudes and abilities required to win and retain power. He had never been obliged to cultivate the skills which this ultimate crisis demanded. He had no experience of identifying and rallying support, forming alliances, seeking compromises, outmanœuvring opposition. He repeatedly made concessions which he did not believe in for tactical reasons. As a result, he was accused of dissimulation at a time when the appearance of integrity was politically essential. Nothing in Louis XVI's life prepared him for the challenge which confronted him in 1788 and thereafter. He was at his most impressive at the end of his life when he had been stripped of public office and was responsible only for his own personal conduct.

In the absence of any clear lead from the Crown, the most vital issue of the day, the election and consequent composition of the Estates-General, became a matter of public debate. The terms of that debate were unwittingly set by the Parlement of Paris. When in September 1788 it registered the edict convening the Estates-General, it added that it should be elected and organized as on the occasion of its last meeting in 1614. The qualification was inserted because the edict was silent on this matter. The judges' long-held fear of ministerial despotism had been intensified by Calonne and Brienne; suspicious, they invoked precedent, the sheet-anchor of any judiciary, in order to prevent the government from rigging the membership of the Estates-General as it had that of the provincial assemblies. When the Parlement took this decision, it may not even have known what the forms of 1614 were. Each of the three orders had been separately represented; there had been an equal number of deputies for each order; and within the Estates-General voting had been by order and not by a head count of the deputies.

The Parlement's decree of September 1788, which was greeted with shock and anger by the patriots, marked the beginning of a new and more intense phase in the political debate. Historians used to interpret the judges' decision as the climax of an aristocratic reaction and the signal for the bourgeoisie, which had up to this point backed the aristocracy, to launch its own revolutionary movement. However, Doyle demonstrated some time ago that the aristocratic reaction was a myth. Egret has produced evidence that, except in a few provinces, most significantly Dauphiné, the bourgeoisie did not support the nobility in the summer of 1788. And Elizabeth Eisenstein has pointed out that, as Mirabeau and Sieyès remarked at the time, the campaign against the Parlement's hapless decision was led by the noble-dominated Society of Thirty, whose members (there were many more than thirty of them) usually met in the house of Adrien Duport, himself a member of the Parlement.

The programme of this campaign was provided by events in Dauphiné where, in the summer of 1788, a noble-led and bourgeois-supported movement in favour of the restoration of the Estates of that province had secured government consent for an assembly which would be elected by the three orders, the clergy, nobility, and the third or rest. But the Third Estate was to have as many representatives as the other two combined and voting was to be by head and not by order in the new assembly. This arrangement was adopted by the Society of Thirty as the model for reforming the Estates-General. It promoted the publication of pamphlets putting forward its case and urged corporate bodies in the provinces to petition the government to accept it. The petitions, which flooded in, demonstrate the moderation of opinion at this time. [**DOCUMENT X**] Nearly all of them limited their requests to the modernization of the Estates-General and universal liability to taxation. The Parlement of Paris rallied to the cause by announcing in December that as there were no fixed rules for the election and composition of the Estates-General, the king could prescribe as he thought fit. But the royal council's decision was ambiguous. It granted the doubling of the Third Estate's representatives but left the question of how votes should be cast in the Estates-General to be settled by the three orders themselves when they met.

b) Polarization of opinion

This partial success resulted in increased political tension because the patriots redoubled their efforts to secure voting by head. The most incisive contribution to the debate came from one of the members of the Society of Thirty, the Abbé Sieyès, whose pamphlet, *What is the Third Estate?*, was published in January 1789. Sieyès argued in a remorselessly abrasive style. Against Rousseau, he held that the General Will can be embodied in elected deputies; that those who so embody it have the authority to endow the nation with a constitution; and that a majority vote of representatives is sufficient to make decisions legitimate. This set of arguments is important because it provided the intellectual justification for the work of the Constituent Assembly. Sieyès also argued, in unbridled polemic, that the members of the nobility were not part of the nation. They were parasites whose privileges set them apart from the useful members of society and who could only join the nation by abandoning those privileges. He was in fact making a powerful case for voting by head; but the effect of his vitriolic rhetoric was to identify the nobility as the enemy of progress from the beginning of the Revolution. His pamphlet provided the Third Estate with its strategy for the Estates-General, but its bold claims and uncompromising language helped to polarize opinion. [**DOCUMENT XI**]

The result of the campaign to secure voting by head, like earlier efforts to establish the principle of equal liability to taxation, was to focus critical attention on the traditional legal distinctions which divided society. This traditional source of social division may have been underrated as a result of the Marxist emphasis on relations of production and class consciousness as the main determinants of social conflict. Revisionist historians have not questioned Marxist criteria for identifying class. On the contrary, their great triumph, the consolidation of the noble and the bourgeois élites into a single dominant class, is based on Marxist criteria. The legal distinctions which separated nobles from commoners may not have been visibly manifested in a national institution since 1614, but they certainly continued to affect public life, particularly in the matter of access to public office. Those with sufficient wealth could buy their way into the nobility. Those with limited means, members of the professional middle class, magistrates in the lower echelons of the judicial hierarchy, lawyers and doctors, had no chance under the Old Regime to make their way up the social and professional ladder. Nor did they have a public forum in which to manifest their dissatisfaction with their circumstances. The elections to the Estates-General presented them with their great opportunity.

The actual electoral arrangements and the results they produced contributed in no small measure to the process of radicalizing and polarizing opinion that was a such a marked feature of 1789. William Doyle's *Origins of the French Revolution* gives a lucid account of very complex procedures. Their political impact can be attributed to three features. First, those who took part in the elections met in assemblies, not only to choose deputies but also to draw up lists of grievances. The elections for the deputies of the Third Estate were indirect, that is, they were held in two or even three stages. Grievance lists were compiled at each stage. This procedure heightened awareness of grievances and encouraged the expectation that they would be remedied. Secondly, the affluent élite was split because the elections were based on legal orders rather than property-ownership and only those with full hereditary nobility were admitted to the second order electoral assemblies. Many thousands of first- and second- generation holders of ennobling office who possessed only personal nobility were, to their intense annoyance, humiliatingly demoted to the Third Estate. Thirdly, the elections gave preponderance in all three orders to those who were not members of the affluent élite. Parish priests (192) greatly outnumbered bishops (51) among the deputies to the first order (303 in all). The second order was dominated by modest country gentry; of the rest, court aristocrats fared better than judges of the parlements. The vast majority of those who participated in the third order elections were peasants and artisans, because all male householders aged twenty-five and over were enfranchised. However, the third order elections were controlled by local lawyers and magistrates who presided over the electoral assemblies, kept the minutes and drew up the grievance lists for their own professional corps and (as seigneurial judges) for village communities. They also dominated the deputies of the Third Estate, of whom 25 per cent were lawyers and 43 per cent office-holders, many of them magistrates of the lower royal courts. No peasants or artisans were sent to Versailles and relatively few businessmen (85, or 13 per cent, of all deputies to the Third Estate).

The grievance lists which these deputies took with them to Versailles are often described as moderate or even conservative, and this is true if the changes they demanded are compared with the changes that were carried out in 1789–90. They certainly did not anticipate the demolition of institutions which occurred as a result of popular rebellion in the summer of 1789. But compared with the past rather than the future, these proposals represented a considerable advance on what even reformist ministers were prepared to offer under the Old Regime. The grievance lists drawn up on behalf of peasant communities and artisan guilds largely reflected their day-to-day problems of earning a living and paying their way. But the general grievance lists, drawn up at the final stage in the electoral process for all orders, reflect political ambitions that went far beyond what the Crown was prepared to concede, even when the Estates-General began. What is most noticeable of all is the large area of common ground shared by the clergy, nobility and Third Estate, all of whom sought what might be broadly described as a liberal regime, with constitutional limits on royal power and guaranteed individual rights. There was a general assumption that the new regime would include regular meetings of the Estates-General, ministerial responsibility, legislation and taxation by consent, provincial estates in all provinces, equal liability to taxation, and the creation of a single national market. Some clerical lists contained reservations about freedom of religion and of expression, some noble lists are silent on equality of opportunity. The most striking issue on which orders disagreed was that which had dominated the political debate since December, namely the procedure to be adopted for voting in the Estates-General. The lists of the First and Second Orders or Estates on the whole favoured voting by order, with some expressing a willingness to be flexible on some issues and in some circumstances. This is consistent with the view that the nobility intended to continue as a separate estate of the realm and retain their honorific if not their useful privileges. The lists of the Third Estate were overwhelmingly committed to voting by head and, by implication, to equality.

c) The stand of the Third Estate

The general conclusion to be drawn from the elections and the grievance lists is that, so far as the deputies to the Estates-General were concerned, absolutism was finished and should be replaced by a liberal regime. There was far less agreement about social change. The opening on 5 May of the Estates-General suggested that the Crown had not accepted the end of absolutism. The statements read on behalf of the king and Necker quite failed to measure up to the occasion. Necker's statement alluded to the possibility of administrative reforms without being specific, bored everyone with detail on the subject of royal finance, and was equivocal on the question of voting procedure. The session ended with instructions that the three orders should withdraw to their three assigned chambers and verify the credentials of deputies. The result was a seven-week strike by the Third Estate. Because the future of France appeared to depend on whether or not the Estates-General was organized as a single assembly voting by head, the Third Estate refused even to verify the credentials of its members except in common with the other two orders. They seized the initiative from the start by inviting the clerical and noble deputies to join them.

The clergy were divided almost equally on this question, a significant proportion (most, but not all, parish priests) identified with the Third Estate. They did not start joining it until 13 June, but meanwhile the knowledge that there was considerable sympathy for their cause among the parish priests undoubtedly strengthened the determination of the Third Estate. The nobles were staunchly opposed to verification of credentials in common: forty-six voted at the start to amalgamate with the Third Estate but were not prepared to go so far as to break ranks. The resistance of the second order during these weeks did much to identify the nobility with reaction. Similar suspicions attached to the Crown which took no bold political initiative to break the deadlock, though it did start concentrating troops in the vicinity of Versailles and Paris.

This raised the stakes. The intransigence of the nobility and the support it was obviously getting from the Crown hardened the attitude of the Third Estate against both. During May and June leaders emerged among the deputies of the Third Estate, Mounier, Barnave, Mirabeau, Sieyès; groups of like-minded deputies who frequented the same cafés coalesced into political caucuses; deputies wrote to their constituents at home to explain what was happening; propagandist news-sheets were published to mobilize public opinion. The Revolution of 1789 differed from all the subsequent revolutions modelled on it precisely because it was the first modern revolution. Those who took part in it had no precedents to guide them. Unlike all the other great revolutions, there was no revolutionary movement or party before the Revolution broke out. There was no programme, no leadership, no identifiable moderate and radical groups. The revolutionaries discovered where they stood, what they wanted, how far they were prepared to go, in response to the events of 1789. That process began in the first weeks of the Estates-General during the stalemate created by the Third Estate's strike and the resistance of the other orders.

That stalemate was broken by votes on 10 June and 17 June when, at the suggestion of Sieyès, the Third Estate issued a final invitation to the other two orders to join it to verify their credentials in common, and then constituted itself as the National Assembly. These votes, which were carried by very large majorities, were technically the beginning of the Revolution because the Third Estate, and the few clergy who had by that stage joined it, knew that they were claiming sovereign power when they assumed the title of National Assembly. The rest of the clergy voted to join the National Assembly on 19 June and lent legitimacy to the Third Estate's coup.

Thereafter the political situation evolved rapidly, largely in reaction to the Crown's maladroit attempts to regain control over events. Necker urged the king to hold a Royal Session, a joint meeting of all three orders, in which he would legitimize the recent actions of the Third Estate by conceding voting by head as part of a package of administrative reforms. Necker's strategy of a Royal Session was adopted. But the programme put forward was changed, thanks to the influence of Artois, Louis XVI's reactionary younger brother, who was able to exert more pressure than usual because the court was in mourning at Marly following the death of the dauphin. The preparations for the Royal Session were clumsy. On 20 June troops excluded the Third Estate from its usual meeting-place without explanation. Fearful that a military coup was under way, the deputies assembled in the nearest large building, a tennis court, where all but one of them took an oath, individually and orally, that they would not be disbanded but would continue to work together to provide France with a constitution. Louis's attempt to reassert control in the Royal Session on 23 June failed. His programme of reforms included all the proposals that had been mulled over for decades, but it allowed the nobility a veto over its own future and ordered separate debates. The decisions of 17 June, to form a National Assembly and vote by head, were annulled instead of being given the royal blessing as Necker intended. The Royal Session failed to win over or intimidate the Third Estate, which held its ground and was joined the next day by the majority of the clergy and many of the nobles. The rest were ordered by the king to join the National Assembly on 27 June.

d) Responsibility and insurrection

The nerve of the deputies of the Third Estate during these seven weeks in May and June is remarkable. Their confidence derived in part from their belief that the financial problems of the monarchy gave them the whip hand. As Mirabeau said, 'The debt is the treasure of the nation.' They assumed that bankruptcy was not a feasible option for the Crown, and they knew that the royal creditors could not be paid unless the Estates-General agreed to fiscal and financial reform. They

were determined to withhold agreement until political reform had
been conceded.

The royal volte-face on 27 June did not signal a change of policy,
it was a means of winning time until reliable foreign regiments could
be moved up to Versailles and Paris. Their presence was intended to
maintain law and order at a time when food was scarce and prices
high, and possibly to intimidate the National Assembly or remove it
to some quiet provincial town. The news of the troop movements and
the dismissal of Necker led to a popular insurrection in Paris on 14
July, during which the Bastille fell to the insurgents. This fortress, a
symbol of tyranny but also a threat to one of the working-class
quarters of the capital, was attacked by a mob in search of weapons.
Its fall was not just symbolic. It indicated that the Crown had in fact
lost control of the capital and the attempt at military repression had
to be abandoned for the time being. The electors of Paris took charge
of the administration of the city and set up a militia, soon to be known
as the National Guard, which was manned by the respectable middle
class and was designed to defend the new political order from military
repression and protect property from mob rule. There were parallel
developments in most provincial towns and cities. A 'municipal revolution' was effected across the length and breadth of France. Existing
town councils were replaced or had new men added to them and
bourgeois militias were set up. They took over from the old centralized bureaucracy and army. Necker was reinstated. The king
visited Paris and, as a gesture of reconciliation, wore the revolutionary
cockade. Emigration of the intransigent nobles, led by Artois, began.

The assumption of political responsibility by middle-class revolutionaries as a result of popular urban insurrection had been no part
of the agenda of the Third Estate when it assembled at Versailles in
May. It was prompted by the Crown's attempt at military repression
and it was facilitated by the harvest failure of the previous year.
Arthur Young remarked in his diary that the friends of the
'Commons' were not displeased with the high price of bread; it
enabled them to mobilize and exploit the discontent of the lower
classes in the towns and it ensured the long-term success of the
National Assembly. One of the most striking features of the Revolution of 1789 is the confidence of the middle-class liberals who led it
that the nation as a whole was behind them. They were not inhibited
in their attacks on absolutism and the nobility by fear of being
overtaken by a more radical, popular revolution, as liberals so often
were in central Europe in 1848. Their confidence rested in part on

their political innocence. They had no dire precedents to alarm and deter them from exploiting popular action. And they were confident that what they sought was not only in the interest of all Frenchmen, but of mankind in general.

Popular insurrection in the towns saved the revolution of the middle class but it did not directly alter its nature. The peasant insurrection did. There was widespread unrest in the French countryside from December 1788 to March 1790, though not in all areas at all times. Its immediate cause was the failure of the harvest of 1788, which resulted in food shortages, high prices, falls in rural employment and incomes. Harvest failure by itself has not been regarded by Marxist historians as an adequate explanation of general peasant rebellion because there had been worse instances of famine in the past without these dramatic results. Hence, Marxists like Labrousse laboured over analyses of economic trends during the half-century before 1789, and were prone to invoke economic conjuncture to explain popular rebellion in town and country. This conjuncture was identified as the failure of the economy to expand at the same pace as the rise in population, which resulted in land hunger in the countryside and a drop in real wages in the towns.

The rate of economic expansion was deemed to have been adequate in the middle decades of the century, but not in the years following the accession of Louis XVI. Agricultural incomes dropped from the late 1770s as a result of a glut in the production of wine, the peasants' chief cash crop. Consequently, the demand for manufactures slackened and unemployment in town and country rose. Economic recovery began around 1786, but was checked by the failure of the harvest in 1788. In an agricultural economy like that of France, the prosperity of the country as a whole depended on the state of the harvest. The peasant revolt was directed specifically against the seigneurial dues, payments in cash or kind which peasants were required to make to whoever owned the right to collect them, whether noble, bourgeois, religious order, or even rich peasant. Seigneurial dues were the target of peasant anger, it was thought, because they were being more intensively exploited in the last years of the eighteenth century, whether by impoverished nobles trying to compensate for economic decline or by bourgeois and well-to-do peasants, who saw them as a business investment.

e) Old explanations challenged

Most of these conclusions have been questioned in recent years. The neo-Malthusian view that population growth was outpacing resources has been undermined by demographic research. This reveals that the French population's growth was modest compared with that of other European countries, and much of the early growth replaced population losses suffered in the seventeenth century. It is also clear that pressure on economic resources was cushioned in the later decades of the eighteenth century by limiting family size. What is now known about the basic conditions of rural existence indicates that the traditional picture of unrelieved misery is misleading. Even agricultural labourers, the rural proletariat, whose numbers were increasing towards the end of the century, often owned a cottage, a garden or small-holding, in some areas a small barn, a cow, sometimes a few sheep. For them, communal grazing rights were vital to their ability to maintain livestock. Defence of those rights, which were being undermined in regions where enclosure had begun, was for them the key issue in the Revolution.

Many earlier assumptions about the seigneurial regime are questionable. The evidence available does not suggest that bourgeois and peasant owners of seigneurial dues levied them more harshly than nobles. There are grave doubts as to whether the seigneurial regime was more intensively exploited towards the end of the eighteenth century, except in Brittany and Burgundy. Seigneurial dues varied considerably, both as a burden on the peasants and as a source of income to seigneurs, from one area to another. What is most important in the context of the Revolution of 1789 is that the peasant risings do not correlate, in their occurrence or their intensity, with regional variations in the seigneurial regime.

No special circumstances have to be adduced to account for peasant hostility towards those who siphoned off part of their surplus. Rents, dues, taxes and tithes were always resented. Such resentment increased in times of harvest failure when unrest and refusal to pay these charges were common. What was different about 1789 was that drawing up the grievance lists encouraged a widespread assumption that seigneurial dues were about to be abolished by a benevolent king. Many peasants anticipated his decision and simply stopped paying them. Some revolts occurred immediately after meetings of village electoral assemblies. Peasants also stopped paying state taxes and clerical tithes in the spring and summer of 1789. In the 'great fear', that bizarre, hysterical, collective panic of late July and early August, triggered by rumours that vagrants had been armed by aristocrats to terrorize the peasants and starve them into submission by destroying the ripening grain, peasants attacked their local châteaux and burned the registers of seigneurial dues. But this was not simply an expression of traditional hostilities. It was a rural manifestation of a general belief that an 'aristocratic plot' or 'aristocratic reaction' could be expected to subvert the work of the National Assembly.

The peasants were able to rebel in 1789 on a scale that had been impossible for over a century because the usual means of repression were lacking. This was the other principal feature of the peasant insurrection of 1789: it was virtually impossible to crush it by force. The authority of the royal administration had been undermined by the revolt of the nobility in 1788 and disappeared altogether following the municipal revolution of 1789. The French regiments in the regular army were unreliable and the revolutionary leadership in the National Assembly was unwilling to call for more reliable units of foreign mercenaries to be used to deal with peasant unrest, knowing that to do so could well be the beginning of a general repression. Only in a few areas were urban militias used against the peasants.

Hence the attempt was made to pacify the peasants by agreeing to what they so obviously wanted, an end to the seigneurial regime. This was proposed by a group of liberal aristocrats in a late-night session of the National Assembly on 4 August 1789. [**DOCUMENT XII**] It precipitated the total destruction of the Old Regime, as deputies, whether carried away by enthusiasm or prompted by malice, voted the end of the tithe, venal offices, municipal and provincial privileges, and voted for appointment to public offices on equal terms. It was the wholesale destruction of all existing institutions on the night of 4 August, not a wilful disregard for tradition and a weakness for simple, abstract ideas, that forced the National Assembly to start from scratch. The reform and amelioration advocated by conservative critics, then and now, were not feasible. The revolutionaries were compelled by what happened in 1789 (the elections to the Estates-General; the resistance of the nobility, backed by the monarchy, to voting by head; the increased militancy of the patriots; and peasant insurrection) to embark on a far more radical programme than anyone had anticipated at the beginning of that momentous year.

Illustrative Documents

DOCUMENT I   Changing evaluations of Alfred Cobban's *The Social Interpretation of the French Revolution* (1968)

Historians, like history, are subject to changing interpretations. Cobban's book, when it was first published, was not seen as a seismic event in the historiography of the Revolution. Betty Behrens pleaded that his book should at least be taken seriously, but even she could not entertain the view that the Revolution was primarily a political event.

(a) *A hostile critic*

Professor Cobban is a skilful debater and he takes visible and gusty delight in scoring points off such eminent historians as Georges Lefebvre and Albert Soboul. . .His principal whipping boy. . .is the statement, familiar to generations of undergraduates, that 'the French Revolution was a bourgeois revolution', and he has a high old time drawing attention to the efforts made by Lefebvre and Soboul to fit groups that they claim to have been bourgeois into standard moulds, to the extent of inventing that oddly named group 'la bourgeoisie rurale', a late-comer in Lefebvre's vocabulary. Much of this is altogether healthy and a very welcome antidote to mechanistic group definitions. . .and we must be thankful to Professor Cobban for having cleaned up some of the litter left as a result of the loose employment of terms.

Even so, Professor Cobban is not averse to using the wicked word himself when it suits his side of the argument. For instance, when in one of his favourite parlour tricks, he attempts to turn the tables on the 'revolutionary bourgeoisie', by suggesting that, far from seeking to destroy the dragon 'feudalism', they did their best to preserve it, then the group, or class, or whatever it is, which the author has been

at such pains to prove never existed as a definable unit is conveniently
reinvented. For Professor Cobban, it seems, the 'bourgeoisie' will do
as a term when applied to a group whose aims were politically and
socially reactionary; it will not do when applied to people who were
attempting to get things changed. As on many occasions in these
lectures, he insists on having the best of both worlds.

Having disposed of the bourgeois revolution he moves on to the
next sacred cow: feudalism. 'The revolutionary bourgeoisie destroyed
feudalism', he quoted Lefebvre and Soboul as rather crudely stating.
This could not be so, for there was no feudalism to be destroyed, and
the distinction between aristocrat and commoner was a political
rather than a social or economic one; to prove his point, the author,
who is much given to verbal definitions, quotes his beloved Burke,
though we are not told why Burke's definition of an English aristocrat
should do for France as well. Here he is on more uncertain ground,
for if the division between the Second and Third Estates was merely
a political one, it is difficult to understand why, long after the Revolution, throughout the Directory and the Consulate, the nobility
should have continued to have been the object of such intense loathing
on the part of the vast majority of the population and why the penal
legislation applying to the émigrés should have been so ruthlessly
maintained. Clearly the French public of that time had not realized
what Professor Cobban, in the 1960s, has discovered, with many arch
chuckles at the expense of French historians: that there was really not
much to the concept of nobility by the end of the eighteenth century,
and that feudalism had long since ceased to exist. It is difficult to
understand why an enemy who was no longer there should have been
pursued with such persistent zeal, why people like Barnave should
have felt such bitter resentment against privilege, when privilege had
become meaningless. . .The trouble with Professor Cobban is that he
goes too far; having set up his Aunt Sally. . .he then goes on not only
to knock it down with a couple of well-aimed verbal lobs, but then
proceeds to offer his own counter-truth: smallholders were in favour
of enclosure, big farmers were opposed to it. We have generally been
told the contrary — the bourgeoisie did not destroy feudalism, but
sought to preserve it, and so on. An ancient tutorial technique says:
'Let us look at it from the other end, let us turn it the other way up.'
Professor Cobban spends much of his time, in these lectures, turning
chairs upside-down and then trying to sit on them. It is an amusing
feat of gymnastics, the audience cannot but applaud his dexterity,
though it may remain unconvinced. In the end, nothing very much

emerges from the conjurer's hat. But perhaps Professor Cobban is merely out to provoke.

Certainly, if only it helps students and historians to be more careful of their definitions and to avoid all-embracing and often meaningless block groups, this little book will have fulfilled a useful purpose. . . But as a criticism of such cautious and meticulous scholars as Lefebvre and Soboul it is often unfair and insufficient. . .It is easy enough to draw attention to and to make fun of the Marxist *coups de chapeau* with which Soboul introduces and closes his chapters ('L'opposition inéluctable entre la bourgeoisie jacobine et le mouvement sansculotte', and so on) — though they are more a formal 'For what we about to receive' and 'For what we have received' than the essence of the work, which is to be found in a detailed and complicated narrative — but these do not detract in any way from his exceedingly balanced judgements on specific issues . . . It is one thing to write one's own history, another to interpret someone else's. Professor Cobban is not only trying to prove that the Revolution was a bad thing for most people. . .he is also implying that historical thought is more important than history, that pirouettes in verbal definitions are more valuable than original research.

('À Bas La Révolution!', *Times Literary Supplement*, 7 January 1965, 8. Reprinted by permission of the author.)

(b) *A defence of Cobban*

. . .Professor Cobban's conclusions would certainly be important if they could be believed. Clearly and soberly set out, well documented and plausible as they are, they have every appearance of being justified, and yet the impression the *Times Literary Supplement*'s reviewer conveys is that they are all either wrong or, as he says, 'old hat'.

. . . For the greater part his weapons are ridicule and sarcasm, and he often directs them against statements which Professor Cobban never made. One of the most conspicuous instances of this is provided by the passage in which he jeers at Professor Cobban for contesting Lefebvre's assertion that the revolutionary bourgeoisie destroyed feudalism. Professor Cobban, he says, believes 'this could not be so for there was no feudalism to be destroyed, and the distinction between aristocrat and commoner was a political rather than a social or economic one: to prove his point [Professor Cobban], who is much

given to verbal definitions, quotes his beloved Burke, though we are
not told why Burke's definition of an English aristocrat should do for
France as well.'

This passage contains more misrepresentations than one would
believe possible in so small a space. In the first place Professor
Cobban did not say that there was no feudalism to destroy in France
in 1789. We may feel he underestimated practices and attitudes dating
back to the middle ages, but all he said was: 'If feudalism in 1789 did
not mean seignorial rights it meant nothing'; he thought it did mean
seignorial rights, but he then went on to point out that these were
often owned by bourgeois who were extremely unwilling to relinquish
them. It is true that he said that the struggle against the nobility was
primarily political, but he said this in a wholly different connexion (à
propos of the counter-revolution) and he did not attempt to prove the
point by quoting Burke. He never quoted Burke at all. The reviewer
misread Burke for Tom Paine and in addition misread Tom Paine's
remark. When Professor Cobban wrote to the *Times Literary Supplement* to protest against these and other errors, the reviewer brushed
his protests aside. 'My apologies to poor Tom,' he said, and then went
on to point out that 'an English definition of aristocracy, whether by
Paine or by Burke, does not necessarily help us to understand the
nature of the French nobility'. Tom Paine, however, in the passage
which Professor Cobban quoted, had not given an English definition
of aristocracy. Even at the second attempt the *Times Literary
Supplement*'s reviewer was unable to bring himself to read what
Professor Cobban had written; for all that Professor Cobban had
quoted Tom Paine as saying was: 'The term Aristocrat is used
here [i.e. in France where he was at the time] similar to the word Tory
in America; — it in general means an enemy of the revolution,
and is used without that peculiar meaning formerly affixed to Aristocracy.'

The *Times Literary Supplement*'s reviewer, in fact, will not take
Professor Cobban seriously. . .He accuses him of being principally
concerned with verbal definitions and debating points. . .

. . .The suggestion that Professor Cobban is merely engaged in
playing a game with words is manifestly unjust; the suggestion, which
is at the root of his reviewer's attack, that he is trying to knock down
a structure he is unable to replace — turning chairs upside-down, as
the reviewer says, and then trying to sit on them — may be unjust in
the sense that no such task of reconstruction could be accomplished
in 170 pages, but has yet to be proved wrong. How comfortable a

repose are Professor Cobban's upside-down chairs likely to provide? When he says in his concluding chapter that though he has been concerning himself with social history he believes the Revolution to have been 'primarily a political revolution', he is drawing a distinction between social and political developments that no one today would accept or could see as providing a foundation for any convincing explanation of the causes and results of the Revolution. Given their traditions, it would not be surprising if the defenders of the orthodoxy, when faced with this statement, were to experience a sense of outrage which made them disinclined to agree.

(Betty Behrens, 'Professor Cobban and His Critic', *The Historical Journal*, 9 (1966), 236–41. Reprinted by permission of the Cambridge University Press.)

(c) *A recent verdict on Cobban*

. . .It is now generally recognized that with Cobban's publication of *The Social Interpretation of the French Revolution* a new era in the historiography of the Revolution has opened. Through the mid 1960s, the long-established 'orthodox' conception recognized in the Revolution an epochal *social* phenomenon — the political expression of fundamental changes in economic conditions and the balance of classes. Historians generally, and not only Marxists, held that the revolution marked the ascendancy of the bourgeoisie as a class, the defeat of a more or less feudal aristocracy, and, hence, the triumph of capitalism. . .

. . .Cobban. . .accepted all the standard scholarship associated with the social interpretation and yet forcefully argued that the social interpretation was inconsistent with it. In particular, he argued, the evidence demonstrated that the French aristocracy was not feudal, the bourgeoisie was not capitalist, and the Revolution itself did not consolidate the triumph of a capitalist society.

Indeed, the new 'revisionist' historiography is to an important extent — but *only* in part — precisely the product of the many decades of increasingly sophisticated and thorough historical research inspired by the social interpretation. Our knowledge of the ancien régime has been impressively expanded by both extensive and highly detailed studies of its social history — further informed by the development of the sub-disciplines of economic, demographic, and regional history. Pre-eminent among the standard bearers of this research was Georges Lefebvre, who had a great deal to do with the nearly universal acceptance of the social interpretation. The breadth and nuances of Lefebvre's own exposition of this interpretation — as most clearly expressed in *The Coming of the French Revolution* — were further enhanced by both admiration for his ground-breaking monographic studies, and respect for his Chair in the History of the Revolution at the Sorbonne. Yet within a few years of Cobban's book, in both France and the English-speaking world, the revisionist approach to the Revolution had simply routed the social interpretation, and gained ascendancy.

This revisionist history, which has by now acquired the status of a 'new international consensus', follows Cobban in arguing that the entire body of social historiography of the ancien régime stands in refutation of the idea of bourgeois class revolution. . .

Virtually all non-Marxist historians have now been won away from the social interpretation, essentially because — ideological issues aside — its supposed historical foundations have simply been found wanting when subjected to scrutiny.

(George C. Comninel, *Rethinking the French Revolution: Marxism and the Revisionist Challenge* (London, 1987), 2–3. Reprinted by permission of the publisher, Verso.)

DOCUMENT II   Indirect taxation: the 'free gift' paid by towns, 1758–87

An edict was issued in August 1758 ordering a 'free gift' to be paid annually by every town in France for a period of six years. The amount required from each was stipulated in the edict, which also authorized the towns to raise the money by means of extra octrois. These were taxes on consumer goods, collected either on entry into the town (wine, hay, wood), or through retailers (meat, bread). This extraordinary wartime tax was levied, not for six years, but until the Revolution, though the amount demanded was cut at the end of the Seven Years War and in 1770 many small towns were discharged absolutely from the obligation to pay it. From 1770 these octrois were collected, not by the towns themselves, but by the Farmers General and thus became a regular indirect tax on towns.

(a) *Taxes to be levied to pay for the 'free gift' authorized by edict in August 1758*

Auxerre: the 'free gift' demanded from this town was 8,000 *livres* p.a. The schedule of taxes authorized to pay it was as follows:[1]

Hogshead of wine	30 sous
Hogshead of beer or cider	15 sous
Hogshead of perry	7 sous 6 deniers
Velte[2] of brandy or liqueur	8 sous
Hogshead of brandy or liqueur	6 livres
Ox or cow	40 sous
Calf, heifer or pig	13 sous 4 deniers
Sheep	5 sous
Cartload of hay or wood drawn by 3 horses	10 sous
Cartload of hay or wood drawn by 2 horses	7 sous 6 deniers
Cartload of hay or wood drawn by 1 horse	5 sous

1. Monetary values: 12 *deniers* (pence) to one *sol* (shilling); 20 *sous* (shillings) to one *livre* (pound).
2. *Velte*: ancient measure, equal to 7-8 *litres*.

(Letters patent, 22 April 1759: Archives Nationales, AD IX 401, 153. Translated by Nora Temple.)

(b) *Royal declaration, 27 July 1765, concerning the municipal* octrois

The expenditure occasioned by the war and the order we propose to bring into the payment of the debts which arose from it and which could not have been foreseen, oblige us to continue for another ten years, from 1 January 1768 to the end of December 1777, the collection of the dues, octrois, and taxes or fixed charges established by several decrees of our council. . .we hope that at the end of the said period of ten years, our financial situation will permit us to suppress all these charges and impositions, half of which we have earmarked for ourselves.[1]

1. The taxes were extended for a further ten years, 1778–87.

(Archives Nationales, AD IX 447B, 28. Translated by Nora Temple.)

(c) *Payments (in* livres*) to be made from 1778 by* pays d'états *in lieu of the 'free gifts' due from the towns in these provinces*

Lille, Douai, Orchers:	223,000
Cambrai:	62,200
Artois:	257,000
Provence:	422,100
Burgundy and Mâconnais:	150,000
Bresse, Bugey and Gex:	25,000
Bigorre:	13,100
Languedoc:	385,000

(Bibliothèque Nationale, AFF 7509.)

DOCUMENT III   Table of loans during Necker's first ministry (in *livres tournois*)

	Capital	Rentes
I. Perpetual rentes (without definite period of amortization):		
Lottery loan of January 1777	18,000,000	720,000 (4%)
Loan of Saint-Esprit, February 1777	9,257,120	462,856 (5%)
Loan of City of Paris, August 1777	7,828,580	391,429 (5%)
	35,085,700	1,574,285
II. Life rentes (government's obligation ends with life on which they are constituted):		
Lottery loan of January 1777	9,800,000	1,090,000
Loan of Saint-Esprit, February 1777	2,042,880	142,144
Loan of city of Paris, August 1977	2,971,420	208,171
Loan of November 1778	48,365,000	4,519,213

	Capital	Rentes
Loan of November 1779	67,150,000	6,571,798
Loan of August 1780	2,216,000	210,854
Loan of February 1781	76,085,900	7,051,539
Loan of March 1781	25,800,000	2,214,540
	234,431,200	22,008,259

III. Royal treasury loans, capital amortized according to terms of loan edict:

	Capital	
City of Genoa, 1776, 1777	7,500,000	
Lottery loan of December 1777	25,000,000	
Lottery loan of October 1780	36,000,000	
Clergy, 1780	14,000,000	
Saint-Esprit, 1780	3,321,143	
	85,821,143	

IV. Loans of the *pays d'états* for the king, amortized:

	Capital	
Burgundy, 1778, 1779	24,200,000	
Languedoc, 1776, 1778, 1779, 1780	48,000,000	
Provence, 1776, 1779	5,437,000	
Artois, 1780	3,000,000	
Brittany, 1779, January 1781	8,535,000	
	89,172,000	

V. Loans from officials and financiers, amortizable at time of abolition of office, interest continues to be paid until debt has been completely liquidated:

	Capital	
Taxi franchise (*privilège des fiacres*)	5,500,000	
Addition to surety bonds of employees of *fermes* and *régies*	24,000,000	

	Capital	*Rentes*
Advances from financiers of *fermes* and *régies* (not anticipations)	5,000,000	
Administrators of gunpowder *régie*	1,000,000	
Chamber of Accounts, Provence	1,000,000	
Loan for repurchase of hundredth tax on offices for eight years	7,000,000	
The *fermes* of Sceaux and Poissy	2,000,000	
	45,500,000	
VI. Increase in amount of anticipations during Necker's ministry	40,000,000	
Total of all loans	530,010,043	

(Robert D. Harris, *Necker, Reform Statesman of the Ancien Regime*
(Berkeley, California, 1979), 134–6. Reprinted by permission
of the Regents of the University of California.)

DOCUMENT IV   Table of Ameliorations, 1776–81

Source of Ameliorations[1]	Annual Savings in Livres Tournois
I. Reorganization of *fermes* and *régies*	
(5) The organization of the *régie générale* in 1777 and the suppression of superfluous offices in the administration of the department of domain and forests.	3,000,000
(6) The reorganization of the three companies in 1780: the farmers-general, the *régie*	

Source of Ameliorations[1]	Annual Savings in Livres Tournois
générale, and the administration of the royal domain	13,700,000
(7) The king's share of profits from the above three financial companies.	1,200,000
(10) The reform of the postal administration . .	2,400,000
(16) Reform of the *régie* of powder by Turgot, which was not included in the *Compte rendu* of Clugny in 1776.	800,000
(27) Restoration by Necker of the *régie* for stagecoaches	1,500,000
(28) Reform of the administration of military supplies for convoys.	1,200,000
Total	23,800,000

II. The government's obligations were being continually amortized during Necker's ministry, this being an important aspect of his credit policy. Whenever the government was liberated from a debt for which it had to make payments in 1776, as recorded by the *Compte rendu* of Clugny, that amount could be added to the list of ameliorations.

(1) The reimbursement of rescriptions of the receivers general, which had been suspended in 1770, during 1776 and 1777 freed the government of obligation in Clugny's *Compte rendu* of 1776	4,200,000
(2) Amortization of capital on rentes paid by the *taille*.	1,800,000
(3) Reimbursement of pensions	1,100,000
(4) Other miscellaneous reimbursements . . .	1,500,000

Source of Ameliorations[1]	Annual Savings in Livres Tournois
(20) The amortization of life rentes due to natural causes during six years, 1776–81 inclusive, and also amortization of exigible loans during the same period. Estimated by Necker as between 9 and 10 million livres. Carried here as	10,000,000
Total	18,600,000

III. Increase of revenue from direct taxes through natural augmentation or by reforms.

(9) Increase of revenue (presumably from the second *brevet* of the *taille* before 1780) and from the capitation to raise money for fodder and supplies for military convoys and for local police and the coast guard . .	3,500,000
(12) Increase of revenue from the *vingtième* in the *pays d'élection* due to Necker's reform of 1777	1,800,000
(13) Increase of revenue from the *vingtième* from *pays d'états*, princes of the blood, frontier clergy, and the Order of Malta	900,000
(14) Reduction of amount permitted for writing off the *vingtième* tax (these had usually been favors granted to high-ranking aristocrats like the duc de Duras at Bordeaux)	800,000
(15) Increase in revenue from administration of the *vingtième* in Paris and the capitation of the court.	700,000
Total	7,700,000

	Annual Savings in Livres
Source of Ameliorations[1]	*Tournois*

IV. (11) A large claim was made by Necker for his reform of pensions, particularly in the payment of those in arrears, which had been a heavy liability in the *Compte rendu* of Clugny. Also included in this figure was liquidation of debts-in-arrears of the king's household   7,200,000

V. (18) Income from the royal lottery founded by Clugny was not included in his *Compte rendu*, as already noted, and after Necker's reform of the administration it yielded annually   7,000,000

VI. The following are a broad range of administrative reforms in several departments, including the suppression of numerous offices considered superfluous.

   (8) Suppression of the offices of numerous treasurers in several departments during 1778 and 1779, and the 48 receivers general in 1780. This increased the annual revenue by   3,500,000

  (17) The profit from the mint had been granted to individuals as a favor under the name of *sur-achat*; Necker discontinued the practice, yielding a saving of   500,000

  (21) Suppression of offices in the king's household and other economies achieved in that department are estimated by Necker as from 2 to 2.5 million livres. Carried here as   2,500,000

  (22) Reform of the foundations for beggars . . .   300,000

  (23) Economy in administration of the lieutenant general of police in Paris.   300,000

Source of Ameliorations[1]	Annual Savings in Livres Tournois
(24) Economy in administration of department of foreign affairs	1,000,000
(25) Income from a tax Clugny had placed on communities but that was not carried in his *Compte rendu* of 1776	1,200,000
(26) An annual expenditure in the *Compte rendu* of Clugny for 'acquisitions and exchanges,' concerning the transfer of royal domain lands. They were in fact nothing but favors given to *grands*, which Necker discontinued	1,500,000
(29) The final article given by Necker included a large variety of savings achieved by reduction or abolition of gratifications, in the reduction of the item of expenditure called 'unforeseen expenditures,' which were often due to ill-considered concessions granted to courtiers. One example of this category may have been Necker's discovery of the pension paid to Maximilien Radix de Sainte-Foy long after it had expired	6,000,000
Total	16,800,000
VII. (19) The final category of the 'free gift of the clergy,' which Necker included as an ordinary revenue, not previously counted as such.	3,400,000

Sources	Amelioration Totals	Livres Tournois
I	. . . .	23,800,000
II	. . . .	18,600,000
III	. . . .	7,700,000
IV	. . . .	7,200,000
V	. . . .	7,000,000

Sources	Amelioration Totals	Livres Tournois
VI	. . . .	16,800,000
VII	. . . .	3,400,000
	Total	84,500,000

1. The twenty-nine articles are arranged in seven categories (designed by roman numerals). The arabic number in parenthesis is the number given by Necker.

(Robert D. Harris, *Necker, Reform Statesman of the Ancien Régime* (Berkeley, California, 1979), 155–9. Reprinted by permission of the Regents of the University of California.)

DOCUMENT V   Extracts from the '*Grandes Remontrances*' of April 1753

These 'Great Remonstrances', the most famous ever drawn up by the Parlement of Paris, demonstrate the judges' strong commitment to the rule of law. Prompted by disputes over the refusal of sacraments (an issue in which they cannot be said to have had any personal, material interest), the judges insist that Louis XV's policy of evoking cases arising from this quarrel to the royal council is a misuse of the royal prerogative. They warn the king that his failure to respect the law and the freedom his subjects enjoy under it is imperilling the very foundation of the monarchy itself.

. . .But our sacred duty is to work for the safety of the State and the preservation of your Crown, to honour the solemn oath we have taken and be worthy of the trust placed in us at all times by the kings your predecessors and by your Majesty. . .

It is the same duty which brings your Parlement to the foot of the throne, to assure your Majesty that the only sure course for the State consists in upholding the fundamental laws of the Monarchy.

A treatise written and published on the order of your august great-grandfather states that: 'The law on which the State is founded establishes a permanent and reciprocal link between the Prince and his descendants on the one hand, and the subjects and their descendants on the other, by a sort of contract which declares that the sovereign should reign and the people obey, . . .a solemn contract by which they give themselves to one another with the aim of helping one another.'

Such has always been, Sire, at the most decisive moments, the language of your Parlement. 'The Kingdom belongs to the King', we said to one of your predecessors, 'and the King belongs to the Kingdom. You are in duty bound to maintain the rights attached to your Crown, which belongs to you and your people together; to you as head and to your people as members of the same body. Subjects owe their Prince devotion and obedience and the Prince owes his subjects protection and defence. Subjects cannot, in any way whatsoever, remove themselves from the obedience they owe their king, and in return the said king must not neglect or abandon them: for in the same way as they owe him loyalty and support, he owes them justice.'

What happy circumstances ensue from this principle! We see contained in it, Sire, the sovereignty of the Prince, his authority over all his subjects equally, as well as the obedience of the people and their legitimate freedom. We see in it these diverse duties brought closely together, and by their union establish the principle of a just monarchy in which the subjects submitting without constraint, find in the authority of their Prince their strength and their security, and in which the Prince, assured of the affection and loyalty of the people, finds in their legitimate freedom his glory and happiness; in which, finally, everything works for the good of the State.

Sire, there is no monarchy which is not endangered by change in one of these duties. . .If obedience fails, the forces of the State are divided and the Kingdom, at war with itself, is ruined. If the legitimate freedom of the people is attacked, their duty still binds them to the State but how different are these links from those forged out of love and trust!. . .

Our privilege, Sire, is to be addressing a Prince who knows that a good king is always loved by his people who justly appreciate the feelings which move the King himself to work for their happiness; who knows also that the principle which guarantees the obedience of the subjects guarantees also their legitimate freedom; that his authority is a fatherly authority and that he reigns to ensure the general good of his state. . .

Thus it is your authority, Sire, which is the strongest support of the legitimate freedom of your subjects, a freedom which makes them submit to you more effectively than constraint would, a freedom, which, equally opposed to licence or servitude, is the characteristic of monarchical government. It is this freedom which makes the people see the Prince as the source of the public good and the keeper of the safety of the State; which ensures the prompt execution of all the orders which the Sovereign's concern for the good of his people causes him to issue, and finally which is the surest guarantee of the stability of the throne, the safety of the Prince and the preservation of his authority.

The laws are the sacred link and are like the seal of this indissoluble agreement. The King, the State and the Law form an indivisible whole. . .Based on the thinking and experience of the greatest kings and the most learned men, aimed only at promoting the good of the State and the true interests of the Prince, only the laws can ensure that the King is not caught unawares, inspire public confidence and thwart those who would disturb the peace of the state, whatever rank or dignity they might hold. No revolution has ever been observed in any state which has not been caused by a change in the laws. Sire, as there is no principle more fundamental than this, there is none more generally accepted. Political thinkers, legal experts, magistrates, kings themselves, all have conceived the idea of a flourishing kingdom only by joining to the obedience of the subjects to the king, the obedience of the King to the Law.

'There are fundamental laws which cannot be changed', said M. Bossuet. 'It is principally of these laws that it is written that by violating them, one shakes the very foundations of the world, after which nothing remains but the fall of empires. It is even a very dangerous thing to alter those laws which are not so fundamental, unless one is forced to do so by some unforeseeable circumstances and with the intention of taking into consideration both the experience of the past and the present situation. An arbitrary government', he also said, 'where the only law is the will of the Prince is not found in well-ordered states; it does not exist in this realm, it is evidently opposed to a legitimate form of government. . .'

From this derives the necessity for the monarchy to establish a body of magistrates entrusted by their function, but more firmly still by the oath they take, with the task of keeping and enforcing all the laws and maxims of the kingdom and to see to their execution, which is their responsibility. . .It is in your name, Sire, that your Parlement watches over the safety of the State; its authority is none other than yours, but it is your authority secure from any sudden dangers, used only for the public good, guided and directed by the laws. Parlement, Sire, is the 'essential minister' of the State, to use the phrase coined by one of our kings, who asked his Parlement to fulfil in his name the promise he

had made at his coronation, to maintain the laws of the kingdom. In
it lies the administration of all that is necessary for the maintenance
and order of public life in your kingdom. This does not alter or
diminish your sovereignty but strengthens it; it is primarily to be
responsible for representing to your subjects your Majesty's very
being, to guarantee them the justice and usefulness of all your laws
and to ensure your Majesty of their loyalty and obedience. . .

Monarchies endure, Sire, only by respecting an unchanging order
in the administration of justice. Having been made by this order
prompt and easily accessible to all your subjects, the administration
of justice renders real and relevant to them the royal majesty which
is so far removed from their eyes by the elevation of the throne. In this
way the people see the Sovereign coming down among them, in a
manner of speaking, to be the defender of the weak, the refuge of the
oppressed, the support of the destitute.

These happy consequences, Sire, are essentially linked to a system
of government as old as monarchy itself, to this gradation of intermediary powers which, subject to the sovereign from which they are
issued and dispersed among the subjects, are the links between the
different parts of the State, maintain your authority without difficulty,
watch over the loyalty of the people whose hearts they conquer by a
constant attention to their needs; sacred vessels in which the
sovereign's authority and the people's trust are united; intermediaries
necessary to establish between the throne and the people this com-
munication which conveys down from the Prince to the people the
protection of justice and the Laws, and up from the people to the
Prince the homage of their respect, their obedience and their love.

Transferring cases to a higher court, Sire, means the destruction of
this political order. Some people want you to believe that this is the
obvious consequence of an absolute authority; but do they not know
that by intercepting and monopolizing these powers which ought to
be dispersed and represent you throughout your kingdom, by sub-
stituting alien forces to the natural forces of this political body they
shake the very foundations of the monarchy?

Give back to the magistrates, Sire, by restoring the procedures
which ancient laws have sanctioned, both the dignity of their function
and their rights to administer justice, which they only desire for the
good of your service and in the interest of justice.

Sire, it is today our sad duty to have to claim back almost all
the basic principles of the constitution of the State, which is a sure
proof of the seriousness of our sad situation. The attack against the

respective rights of the Peers and the Parlements of which they are members, by a transfer of cases to a higher court which, by an unlawful procedure destroys the strongest and most ancient institution, finally proves the shattering effect which the schism is capable of causing in all the orders of the monarchy.

> (J. Flammermont, *Remontrances du Parlement de Paris au XVIIIe siècle* (3 vols., Paris, 1888–95), vol. 1, 522–8, 568–9, 581. Translated for this volume by Hélène Impey.)

DOCUMENT VI Extracts from other remonstrances of the Parlement of Paris

(a) *The Parlement claims that verification of royal laws by the parlements is part of the fundamental laws: extract from the remonstrances of 27 November 1755*

It is out of loyalty to you, Sire, that we repeat what your Parlement respectfully said to one of your predecessors, through the First President: 'We have, Sire, two kinds of laws: on the one hand the King's ordinances which can be altered according to changes in time and circumstance; on the other hand, the laws of the Kingdom which are inviolable, by which you ascended to the throne and this crown has been preserved by your predecessors. Among these public laws, one of the most holy and which your predecessors have religiously kept is never to publish any law and ordinance without having it verified by their parlement; they judged that breaking that law was also breaking the law by which they are made kings, and would give their people reason to doubt their good intention. . .'

It is from one of your predecessors, whose recent reign has left in the whole of France a strong impression of respect and love, that the State has been again entrusted so to speak with the keeping of this ancient rule, that the 'conservation and maintenance of the laws belong naturally to Parlement. . .'

> (J. Flammermont, *Remontrances du Parlement de Paris au XVIIIe siècle* (3 vols., Paris, 1888–95), vol. 2, 69–70. Translated for this volume by Hélène Impey.)

(b) *Doctrine of the unity of all the parlements: remonstrances of the Parlement of Paris, 22 August 1756*

The assemblies of higher magistrates known as Parlements constitute the ancient court of the King, originally part of his suite and eventually settled in the capital. The Paris Parlement is the highest and metropolitan court of the Realm, to use the phrase of King Francis I. All the others are branches of it, or better, extensions of it. So the metropolitan court and all its colonies are the various classes of the one single parlement, the various members of one single body, moved by the same spirit, based on the same principles, devoted to the same purpose.

From this derives, Sire, this consensus of all your parlementary courts when it is a question of defending your interests; from this their unanimous reactions, their spontaneous agreement, their actions, similar without being previously agreed, employed in the repression of anything which endangers your authority, threatens the laws of the Realm, of any innovation likely to upset the Church or the State; from this also derives, as an unavoidable consequence, the hatred which your parlement has always aroused in the hearts of those who have attempted to alter the principles on which is based the government of France and replace them with new ones.

. . .[W]e cannot remain silent on an even more important subject which relates directly to the constitution of the State; it is the plan which seems to have been considered to dissolve the whole body of magistrates in France. How could we, Sire, conceal our well-justified fears on such an important subject? Everything points to this ruinous deadly plan, everything makes it seem inevitable. . .

The monarch, the law, the magistrates constitute a whole which cannot be divided: the monarch whose role is to govern as a legislator and a father, the law which exists to establish rules and trust, the magistrates who maintain authority, justice and obedience by their example and the execution of the laws.

It is this sacred and indissoluble union which is the foundation of all justice and order. The body of magistrates cannot be destroyed except by subverting the law, and if there is no law, what becomes of the King's authority?

(J. Flammermont, *Remontrances du Parlement de Paris au XVIIIe siècle* (3 vols., Paris, 1888–95), vol. 2, pp. 138–46. Translated for this volume by Hélène Impey.)

(c) *The Parlement defends the rule of law: remonstrances of the Parlement of Paris, 24 June 1763*

The King, the State, and the Law are an indivisible whole; in the same way as the sovereign is the author and the guardian of the laws, so the laws are the foundation and the guarantee of the authority of the Sovereign; thus any attack on the laws affects more or less directly the Sovereign himself; to ignore the existence or the irrefutable force of the laws which are by their very nature unchanging and the basis for the conduct of the State, would be endangering the strength of the throne. . .

. . .The need to have laws verified by Parlement is one of the unchanging laws of the kingdom, one of these laws which cannot be violated without violating the law by which the kings themselves are kings, without casting doubt on the power and sovereignty of your Majesty. . .

> (J. Flammermont, *Remontrances du Parlement de Paris au XVIIIe siècle* (3 vols., Paris, 1888–95), vol. 2, 342–4. Translated for this volume by Hélène Impey.)

DOCUMENT VII The king upholds his conception of sovereignty: Louis XV's 'Flagellation Speech', 3 March 1766

Louis's verbal whipping of the Parlement of Paris was occasioned by that court's intervention in the major conflict then going on between the Crown and the Parlement of Rennes (the Brittany affair) and the judges' claim that the thirteen parlements constituted a single entity. More generally the king's speech was a response to the judges' assertions (sustained for more than a decade) that the monarchy was subject to constitutional limitations of which the parlements were guardians. The immediate shock caused by Louis's dramatic initiative soon wore off: by March 1768 the Parlement of Paris was again presenting remonstrances on the Brittany affair.

What has happened in my parlements of Pau and Rennes is of no concern to my other parlements; I have dealt with these courts as befitted my authority, and I answer to no one.

I would make no other reply to the many remonstrances presented to me on this subject, if their coincidence, their offensive style, the recklessness with which they put forward the most inaccurate principles and the unheard-of language used to express them did not demonstrate the damaging effects of that unity of action which I have already forbidden, which people wish to establish in principle even if they dare not implement it in practice.

I shall not tolerate the formation in my kingdom of an association which would cause the natural bond created by similar duties and common reponsibilities to degenerate into a league for resistance, nor the introduction of a fictitious body into the monarchy which could only shatter its harmony; the magistracy is not a corps, nor is it an order distinct from the three orders of the realm; the magistrates are my officers charged with carrying out on my behalf the truly royal task of administering justice to my subjects, a function which attaches them to my person and for which I will always esteem them. I understand the importance of their services; it is therefore a fallacy, which can only tend to shake confidence by spreading false alarms, to imagine that a plan has been drawn up to annihilate the magistracy, or to suppose that it has enemies close to the throne; its only real enemies are those within it who persuade it to adopt a language opposed to its principles; who encourage it to claim that the parlements form one and the same body, divided into several branches; that this body, necessarily indivisible, is the essence and foundation of the Monarchy; that it is the seat, the tribunal and the voice of the nation; that it is the guardian and indispensable trustee of its liberties, interests and rights. . . To try to make such pernicious novelties into principles is to harm the magistracy, to deny the reasons for its existence, to betray its interests and to repudiate the veritable fundamental laws of the state; as if anyone could forget that sovereign authority is vested in my person alone,. . . that the existence and authority of the law courts are derived from me alone;. . . that legislative power belongs to me alone, unqualified and undivided; that it is on my authority alone that the officers of my courts proceed, not to the framing, but to the registration, publication and execution of the law. . .; that I am the source of public order, and that the rights and interests of the Nation, which some dare envisage as an entity separate from the monarch, are at one with my rights and interests, and are in my hands alone. . .

Remonstrances will always be welcome when they reflect that moderation which is appropriate to the magistracy and the truth, when they are confidential and respect what is proper and suitable, when these communications, so wisely ordained, are not transformed into malicious attacks, in which submission to my will is treated as a crime, and the execution of the duties I have prescribed as a matter of shame; in which it is suggested that the whole of the Nation groans to see its rights, its liberty, its security about to perish under the onslaught of a dreadful power, and in which it is claimed that the bonds of obedience are about to be broken; but if, after I have considered such remonstrances and knowing what is at stake I hold to my intention, the courts persevere in their refusal to submit to it, instead of proceeding to register according to the express command of the king. . . if they attempt to annul on their own authority laws which have been solemnly registered, and if finally, after I have been compelled to use my authority to its full extent, they dare to continue resisting it, by whatever means. . . and confusion and anarchy subvert legitimate order, then the scandalous spectacle of an opposition challenging my sovereign power would, unhappily, force me to use all the power I have received from God to protect my people from the dire consequences of such attacks. . .

> (J. Flammermont, *Remontrances du Parlement de Paris au XVIIIe siècle* (3 vols., Paris, 1888–95), vol. 2, 556–8. Translated by Nora Temple.)

DOCUMENT VIII   Amelot de Chaillou, intendant of Dijon, opposes the implementation in Burgundy of Laverdy's municipal reform of 1764–5

Intendants' powers over towns were significantly diminished by this reform. In Burgundy it was opposed by the provincial estates too, but welcomed by the Parlement of Dijon, whose authority it would have enhanced. Amelot de Chaillou thwarted the implementation of the reform in Burgundy by allying with the provincial estates.

(a) *Amelot to Laverdy, 26 December 1766*

. . . I hope that this province will seem to you to merit the same preferential treatment as Languedoc, since its administration is founded on very similar principles. . . I should be failing in my duty if I did not contradict what some have ventured to assert to you concerning the particular satisfaction that the towns of Auxerre, Bar-sur-Seine and Mâcon feel about the implementation of the edicts of 1764 and 1765. I can and should assure you of what has perhaps been kept from you, that these three towns have not ceased to be troubled by agitation and dissension, that the inhabitants are given over to cabals, spite and bitter hatred and never-ending litigation.

(Archives Nationales, H(1) 144, 5. Translated by Nora Temple.)

(b) *Laverdy to Amelot, 28 January 1767*

He acknowledges receipt of Amelot's lengthy memorandum on the privileges of the province of Burgundy, but it is not what he sought.

I asked for your advice on how the edicts of 1764 and 1765 concerning the election of municipal officials and the administration of towns might be adapted to Burgundy and all you send me is criticism of these laws. . . leaving aside the fact that the public satisfaction which the inhabitants of towns in other provinces of the kingdom where these edicts are being implemented shows the advantages which ought to result from them. . . the people of the province of Burgundy, Bresse, etc., are asking for these edicts, and they complain about the arbitrary way in which these towns are now governed, I have evidence of this piling up in my office. . .

He will not comment on Amelot's detailed criticism of the draft declaration that had been drawn up for Burgundy.

. . . The document you have commented on has been so mutilated and changed that I hardly recognized the draft which I sent last year to the provincial Estates, so I am certainly not going to defend it. All I will say on this matter is that the draft which was sent to the Estates was approved by them, and they have agreed that they will themselves seek the support and approval of M. le Prince de Condé [governor of the province].

(Archives Nationales, H(1) 144, 8. Translated by Nora Temple.)

DOCUMENT IX   List of ministers, 1743–89

Chancelier *(Chancellor)*

Head of the judicial system and the most senior of the officers of the Crown. The long periods which Chancellors served in office are misleading. The Chancellor was irremovable and could not be dismissed if he lost the confidence of the king. If he refused to resign, as did Maupeou after 1774, he retained the office but a Keeper of the Seals was appointed to perform its functions.

1717–50 Henri-François d'Aguesseau
1750–68 Lamoignon de Blancménil
1768–90 Réné-Nicolas-Charles-Augustin de Maupeou

Compare: 1635–72 Séguier; 1674–77 d'Aligre; 1677–85 Le Tellier; 1685–99 Boucherat; 1699–1714 Phelypeaux.

Garde des Sceaux *(Keeper of the Seals)*

1750–7 Machault d'Arnouville
1761–2 Berryer (also Secretary of State for the Navy)
1763–8 Feydeau de Brou
1774–87 Miromesnil
1787–8 Lamoignon de Basville
1788–9 Barentin
1789–90 Champion de Cicé

Compare: 1633–5 Séguier; 1652–6 Molé; 1672 d'Aligre; 1718–20 de Paulmy.

Contrôleur Général des Finances *(Controller-General)*

The key domestic minister, responsible for finance and the economy.

1740–5 Orry
1745–54 Machault d'Arnouville
1754–6 Moreau de Séchelles
1756–7 Peirenc de Moras
1757–9 Boullongne
1759 (March–November) Silhouette
1759–63 Bertin
1763–8 Laverdy
1768–9 Maynon d'Invau
1769–74 Terray

1774–6   Turgot
1776 (May–October) Clugny
1776–7   Taboureau des Reaux, with Necker as Director of the Royal
         Treasury
1777–81 Necker, with the title of Director General of Finances
1781–83 Joly de Fleury
1783 (April–October) d'Ormesson
1783–7   Calonne
1787   Bouvard de Fouqueux
1787   Laurent de Villedeuil
1787-90 Lambert

Compare: 1661–83 Colbert; 1683–9 Le Pelletier; 1689–99 Phelypeaux; 1699–1708 Chamillart; 1708–15 Desmaretz.

Secretary of State for Foreign Affairs

1737–44 Amelot de Chaillou
1744–7   marquis d'Argenson
1747–51 Brulart de Sillery, vicomte de Puisieux
1751–4   Barberie de Saint-Contest
1754–7   Rouillé
1757–8   Bernis
1758–61 Choiseul
1761–70 Choiseul and his cousin, duc de Praslin
1771–4   d'Aiguillon
1774–87 Vergennes
1787–90 Montmorin

Compare: 1663–71 Lionne; 1671–9 Pomponne; 1679–96 Colbert de Croissy; 1696–9 Pomponne; 1699–1716 Colbert de Torcy.

Secretary of State for War (also responsible for the frontier provinces)

1743–57 comte d'Argenson
1757–8   de Paulmy
1758–61 Belle-Isle
1761–70 Choiseul

1771–4 Monteynard
1774–5 Muy
1775–7 Saint-Germain
1777–80 Montbarrey
1780–7 Ségur
1788–9 Puységur

*Compare: 1643–77 Le Tellier; 1662–91 Louvois; 1691–1701 Bar-
bezieux; 1701–9 Chamillart; 1709–15 Voisin.*

*Secretary of State for the Navy (also responsible for colonies
and commerce)*

1723–49 Maurepas
1749–54 Rouillé
1754–7 Machault d'Arnouville
1757–8 Peirenc de Moras
1758   Massiac
1758–61 Berryer
1761–6 Choiseul
1766–70 Praslin
1771–4 Bourgeois de Boynes
1774   Turgot
1774–80 Sartine
1780–7 de Castries
1787–90 La Luzerne

*Compare: 1669–83 Colbert; 1683–90 Seignelay; 1690–9 L. Phely-
peaux; 1699–1715 J. Phelypeaux.*

*Secretary of State for the Royal Household (also responsible
for religious affairs,* pays d'états, *interior provinces, and the
city of Paris)*

1718–49 Maurepas
1749–75 Saint-Florentin, duc de La Vrillière
1775–6 Lamoignon de Malesherbes
1776–83 Amelot de Chaillou
1783–7 Breteuil
1787–9 Villedeuil

Compare: 1643–68 du Plessis; 1668–83 Colbert; 1683–90 Seignelay; 1690–3 L. Phelypeaux; 1693–9 J. Phelypeaux; 1699–1718 L. Phelypeaux, marquis de La Vrillière.

DOCUMENT X   The election and composition of the Estates-General: a view from the provinces

The mayor, aldermen and councillors of Bourges, capital town of the province of Berry in central France, together with deputies from all the professional bodies and guilds in the town, held a general assembly on 18 December 1788. This meeting, which was more representative than municipal assemblies normally held in the town, seems to have been a spontaneous response to the decision to summon the Estates-General and the call of the Society of Thirty for petitions. One of the magistrates of the bailliage *court took the chair. In the absence of the mayor of Bourges, who was in Versailles attending the Assembly of Notables, the first alderman opened the discussion. He began by praising Louis XVI, who had remitted the subventions traditionally paid to kings on their accession to the throne, abolished* mainmorte *on the royal domains, led the nation in a useful and honourable war and had now decided to consult the nation about the work of reform. But he went on to argue that they would be lacking in their duty towards the king and themselves if they did not protest against the proposed composition of the Estates-General (as nearly all the towns in the kingdom had done) and appeal to the king to protect the Third Estate.*

The Third Estate undoubtedly forms the largest part of the nation; it is that which pours into the coffers of the king the greater part of the taxes which are the nerves of the state; it is that which composes, renews and augments the many and loyal troops which are its safeguard. Its influence in society, by the larger number of individuals which compose it, by the abundance and variety of its riches, by the extent of its understanding, and by the considerable mass of its landed property, sufficiently justifies the legitimate right of this order to have a representation greater in extent than that which it had in earlier Estates-General, and notably in that of 1614.

The existence of the Third Estate has not always been what it is today, it has for long groaned in the chains of servitude and under the oppression of feudal government. Restored to liberty by the benevolence and protection of its kings, its strength has only gradually reached maturity. In the time of former Estates-General, such as that of 1614, it was still weak; the nobility and the clergy diminished it; therefore it had few representatives, and the greater part of these were chosen from the nobility.

Today, on the contrary, the Third Estate is the centre of knowledge and the arts, it includes a numerous body of farmers and merchants whose industry and energy are the principal source of the wealth of the state, and it more than ever deserves the care and protection of the sovereign: so we see that our august monarch in granting a provincial administration [refers to the provincial assembly of Berry instituted by Necker in 1778] wished that the deputies of the Third Estate should be equal in number to those of the other orders combined, and this has been extended to the other provincial administrations, and even to the estates of the province of Dauphiné created since. . .

The Assembly agreed:

that the number of deputies for each province should be in proportion to its size, wealth and population;

that the Third Estate, comprising forty-nine fiftieths of the nation, and carrying, unjustly, nearly all its expenses, should now and always be represented in the Estates-General by a number of deputies greater than those of the clergy and nobility combined, so that the influence of the Third Estate in the Estates-General should be at least equal to that of the other two orders combined;

that the deputies of the Third Estate should always be elected by their peers and chosen from the citizens of the same order in a meeting free and independent of all outside influence; the said deputies to be mandated by those who elect them;

that the nomination of electors or deputies be effected by free votes and secret ballot.

[The minutes of the meeting were signed by 61 persons.]

(Archives municipales, Bourges, BB29. Translated by Nora Temple.)

DOCUMENT XI Extract from *What is the Third Estate?*, by the Abbé Sieyès, January 1789

Originally from the south but educated in Paris, Sieyès (1748–1836) was beginning to make his mark in the administrative hierarchy of the diocese of Chartres in the 1780s and to acquire some 'political' experience in national and provincial assemblies of the French clergy. He played a key role in the early months of the Revolution and in the events which brought Napoleon to power in November 1799. In the extract that follows, Sieyès assumes the unity of the Third Estate and stresses the gulf between it and the nobility.

Chapter 1: The Third Estate is a Complete Nation

What does a nation require to survive and prosper? It needs *private* activities and *public* services.

These private activities can all be comprised within four classes of persons:

1) Since land and water provide the basic materials for human needs, the first class, in logical order, includes all the families connected with work on the land.

2) Between the initial sale of goods and the moment when they reach the consumer or user, goods acquire an increased value of a more or less compound nature through the incorporation of varying amounts of labour. In this way human industry manages to improve the gifts of nature and the value of raw material may be multiplied twice, or ten-fold, or a hundred-fold. Such are the activities of the second class of persons.

3) Between the production and the consumption, as also between the various stages of production, a variety of intermediary agents intervene, to help producers as well as consumers; these are the dealers and the merchants. Merchants continually compare needs according to place and time and estimate the profits to be obtained from warehousing and transportation; dealers undertake, in the final stage, to deliver the goods on the wholesale and retail markets. Such is the function of the third class of persons.

4) Besides these three classes of useful and industrious citizens who deal with *things* fit to be consumed or used, society also requires a vast number of special activities and of services *directly* useful or pleasant to the person. This fourth class embraces all sorts of occupations, from the most distinguished liberal and scientific professions to the lowest of menial tasks.

Such are the activities which support society. But who performs them? The Third Estate.

Public services can also, at present, be divided into four known categories, the army, the law, the Church and the bureaucracy. It needs no detailed analysis to show that the Third Estate everywhere constitutes nineteen-twentieths of them, except that it is loaded with all the really arduous work, all the tasks which the privileged order refuses to perform. Only the well-paid and honorific posts are filled by members of the privileged order. Are we to give them credit for this? We could do so only if the Third Estate was unable or unwilling to fill these posts. We know the answer. Nevertheless, the privileged have dared to preclude the Third Estate. 'No matter how useful you are', they said, 'no matter how able you are, you can go so far and no further. Honours are not for the like of you. . .'

. . . It suffices to have made the point that the so-called usefulness of a privileged order to the public service is a fallacy; that, without help from this order, all the arduous tasks in this service are performed by the Third Estate; that without this order the higher posts would be infinitely better filled; that they ought to be the natural prize and reward of recognised ability and service; and that if the privileged have succeeded in usurping all well-paid and honorific posts, this is both a hateful iniquity towards the generality of citizens and an act of treason to the commonwealth.

Who is bold enough to maintain that the Third Estate does not contain within itself everything useful to constitute a complete nation? It is like a strong and robust man with one arm still in chains. If the privileged order were removed, the nation would not be something less but something more. What then is the Third Estate? All; but an 'all' that is fettered and oppressed. What would it be without the privileged order? It would be all; but free and flourishing. Nothing will go well without the Third Estate; everything would go considerably better without the two others.

It is not enough to have shown that the privileged, far from being useful to the nation, can only weaken and injure it; we must prove further that the nobility is not part of our society at all: it may be a *burden* for the nation, but it cannot be part of it.

. . . Such a class, surely, is foreign to the nation because of its *idleness*.

The nobility, however, is also a foreigner in our midst because of its *civil and political* prerogatives.

What is a nation? A body of associates living under *common* laws and represented by the same *legislative assembly*, etc.

Is it not obvious that the nobility possesses privileges and exemptions which it brazenly calls its rights and which stand distinct from the rights of the great body of citizens? Because of these special rights, the nobility does not belong to the common order, nor is it subjected to the common laws. Thus its private rights make it a people apart in a great nation. It is truly *imperium in imperio*.

As for its *political* rights, it also exercises these separately from the nation. It has its own representatives who are charged with no mandate from the People. Its deputies sit separately, and even if they sat in the same chamber as the deputies of ordinary citizens they would still constitute a different and separate representation. They are foreign to the nation first because of their origin, since they do not owe their powers to the People; and secondly because of their aim, since this consists in defending, not the general interest, but the private one.

The Third Estate then contains everything that pertains to the nation while nobody outside the Third Estate can be considered as part of the nation. What is the Third Estate? *Everything*!

(Emmanuel Joseph Sieyès, What is the Third Estate?, translated by M. Blondel, ed. by S.E. Finer, introduction by Peter Campbell (London, 1963). Reprinted by permission of Professor Finer.)

DOCUMENT XII   The night of 4 August 1789: an account of the proceedings of the National Assembly.

Etienne Dumont was one of four Genevans who collaborated with Mirabeau (drafting speeches, editing his newspaper, supplying him with material on financial and other topical issues), doing whatever they could to ensure that his ambition to become first minister was realized, in the hope that if he came to power he would withdraw French troops from Geneva (introduced in 1782 to prop up the old oligarchical regime) and facilitate the introduction of more representative institutions. Dumont's memoirs are an important source for the early liberal phase of the Revolution.

But if the Assembly lost a lot of time in discussing the rights of man, it certainly made up for it during the night session of 4 August. Never was so much business accomplished in so short a time. What needed a year's care and attention was proposed, discussed, voted, decided by general acclamation. I do not know how many laws were decreed: the abolition of feudal dues, the abolition of the tithe, the abolition of provincial privileges, three matters which by themselves alone embraced a whole system of jurisprudence and policy, were decided, along with ten or twelve others, in less time than it takes in the English Parliament for the first reading of a bill of any importance. You could compare the assembly to a dying man who makes his will in haste, or to put it better, each liberally gave away that which did not belong to him, and took pride in being generous at the expense of others.

I witnessed this unexpected scene, which Sieyès and Mirabeau, and several other leading deputies, missed.

It began with a report on the unrest in the provinces, of châteaux in flames, gangs of bandits attacking the nobility and devastating the countryside. The duc d'Aiguillon, Noailles, and several others of the noble minority, after these accounts of disaster, declared that only a great act of generosity could calm the people, and that it was time to abandon odious privileges and let them feel the benefits of the revolution. I don't know what excitement got hold of the Assembly. There was no longer any calm or calculation. Each in turn proposed a sacrifice, brought a new offering to the altar of the fatherland, divested himself or divested others. There was no chance to reflect, object, ask for time; an emotional contagion seized their hearts. This renunciation of all privileges, this abandonment of so many rights that were a burden on the people, this multitude of sacrifices had an air of magnanimity which led one to forget the indecency of this impetuosity and haste so unsuitable in legislators. That night I saw good and brave deputies who cried for joy to see the work advanced so quickly, finding themselves swept along, minute by minute, on the wings of an enthusiasm which exceeded all their hopes. It is true that not everyone was carried along by the same sentiment. Many a one who felt ruined by a proposition which had just been carried unanimously, proposed another for revenge so as not to suffer alone; but the Assembly as a whole was not privy to the intentions of those who started the debate and they advanced their cause by profiting from this kind of general intoxication. The renunciation of provincial privileges was made by their respective deputies; those from Brittany were mandated to uphold theirs and were as a result more embarrassed than the rest; but they came forward as a group, and declared that they would use all their efforts with their constituents to get them to ratify the renunciation of privileges. This great and proud operation was necessary to make a political unit of a monarchy which was formed piecemeal by aggregating several states, each of which had preserved some ancient rights, some special privileges, a form of constitutional order which had to be destroyed to found a single body capable of receiving a single Constitution.

The next day people began to reflect on what had been done and there was discontent on all sides. Mirabeau and Sieyès, each for his own reasons, rightly condemned the follies of this enthusiasm. 'Just like the French', said the first, 'to spend an entire month arguing about syllables and in a night they overthrow all the ancient order of the monarchy.' The decree on tithes annoyed Sieyès more than all the rest. In the sessions which followed the deputies deluded themselves that they could amend and modify what had been most imprudent in these precipitate decrees; but it was not easy to retract concessions which the people already regarded as indisputable rights. Sieyès made a speech that was vigorous and sound. He pointed out that to abolish the tithe without indemnity was to rob the clergy of their property and to enrich proprietors; because each having bought his property at a price which allowed for the tithe, found himself at a stroke enriched by a tenth as a free gift. It was this speech, which it was impossible to refute, that he ended with this phrase, so often quoted: 'They wish to be free, but they do not know how to be just.'

(Etienne Dumont, *Souvenirs sur Mirabeau et sur les deux premières Assemblées Legislatives* (Paris, 1832), 142–7. Translated by Nora Temple.)

Glossary

ASSEMBLY OF NOTABLES. A gathering of the leaders of corporate bodies — parlements, provincial estates, city councils, Catholic church — summoned by the king (who nominated its precise membership) to lend support to measures put forward by the government. Its failure to provide effective backing in 1626–7 to reforms proposed by Richelieu led to its demise until it was resuscitated by Calonne in 1787.

BOURGEOISIE DE ROBE. Collective term for the judges in the lesser royal law courts (*bailliage, sénéchaussée, présidial*) who, unlike their seniors in the parlements (collectively known as the *noblesse de robe*) did not enjoy noble status. Friction between the two sets of magistrates over the attributions of their respective courts was exploited by Lamoignon in 1788. The *bourgeoisie de robe* was the highest rank in the Third Estate and in 1789 provided much of its political leadership.

CAPITATION. A graduated poll tax introduced in 1695, suppressed in 1698, re-established in 1701. It was estimated in the late eighteenth century to represent about 9 per cent of a peasant's income, 1 per cent of a noble's income.

CONTROLLER-GENERAL. *Contrôleur général des finances.* The minister responsible for royal finance and the economy. From the time of Colbert (1665–83) the key government minister.

DIXIÈME. Literally, a tenth. Forerunner of the *vingtième* tax and like it a tax (in theory) on all incomes, but levied only in wartime, 1710–17, 1733–7, 1741–9.

ESTATES-GENERAL. A national representative body whose convocation was at the king's discretion. It fell into desuetude after the 1614–15 meeting, largely because, unlike the British Parliament, it did not control the government's revenue.

FARMERS GENERAL. A syndicate of 40–60 financiers who paid

the Crown an annual lump sum for the right to collect indirect taxes and to manage the salt and tobacco monopolies; they ran the most efficient and hated fiscal organization in France.

FRONDE. Literally, 'sling' or 'catapult'; historically, the civil war (1648–52) which occurred during Louis XIV's minority. It pitted the Crown (represented by the Queen Mother, Anne of Austria, and Cardinal Mazarin) against the parlements and the great aristocrats, who included some of the king's close relatives.

GALLICANISM. An ecclesiastical ideology which purported to protect the Catholic Church in France against abuse of papal power by exalting the administrative and disciplinary powers of the French king and bishops at the expense of the Pope and subordinating the latter's authority in matters of doctrine to that of a general council of the Church. The chief tenets of Gallicanism were defined in four propositions voted by the Assembly of French Clergy in 1682.

GÉNÉRALITÉS. The thirty-four administrative divisions of France, each one headed by an intendant and by a *bureau des finances* staffed by *trésoriers généraux de France*. In *pays d'élections* the *généralité* was subdivided into *élections* staffed by *élus* who were responsible, under the supervision of the intendant, for the levy of direct taxes.

GRIEVANCE LISTS. *Cahiers de doléances.* Lists of complaints and suggestions for reform drawn up by electoral assemblies in the spring of 1789 as part of the process of electing the Estates-General.

INTENDANT. The most important agent of royal government in the provinces with almost unlimited authority within his area of jurisdiction, the *généralité* (see above), but particularly active in implementing fiscal and economic policy. Not a venal official but the holder of a commission that could be revoked if the intendant was ineffectual.

LETTRE DE CACHET. A simple sealed letter signed by the king conveying his instructions in respect of particular individuals or cases; acquired a generally sinister reputation because it was used to exile or imprison without charge or trial those who opposed the Crown.

LETTRE DE JUSSION. Letter from the king to a parlement ordering judges to register edicts they disliked. Continued defiance led to a *lit de justice*.

LIT DE JUSTICE. Literally 'bed of justice'. A special session of the

Parlement of Paris attended by the king to enforce registration of edicts and overrule the opposition of the judges. *Lits de justice* in provincial parlements were presided over by a personal representative of the king.

LIVRE, SOL (pl. 'SOUS'), DENIER. Literally 'pound', 'shilling', 'penny'. Money of account whose ratios were exactly like those of Britain's pre-metric currency: 12 *deniers* to a *sol*, 20 *sous* to a *livre*.

ORDERS and ESTATES. French society was legally divided into three orders categorized by function and rank: the first order, the clergy; the second order, the nobility; the third order, the rest, those who were neither clerics nor nobles. Estates (provincial and general) were assemblies of deputies representing the three orders.

PACTE DE FAMINE. Literally 'famine plot'. Food shortages were often popularly attributed to deliberate hoarding by merchants, or even government ministers, intent on making a profit from the inflated prices occasioned by dearth.

PARLEMENT. A law court, not a parliament as in Britain. There were thirteen parlements in France, senior royal courts of appeal, of which the most important was the Parlement of Paris. They were politically important because in addition to their judicial functions they had wide administrative powers which often brought them into conflict with the local intendants, and royal edicts could not be implemented within the jurisdiction of a parlement until it had registered them.

PAYS D'ÉTATS. Provinces (notably Brittany, Burgundy, Languedoc) in which estates, assemblies representative of the three legal orders, had survived and were in charge of the collection of direct taxes. They could therefore negotiate favourable terms with the Crown and their tax burden was relatively lighter than that of other provinces, the *pays d'élections*, where direct taxes were collected by royal officials.

REMONSTRANCE. *Remontrance*. Formal protest presented by the parlement to the king explaining its objections to a royal edict or decree sent to it for registration.

RENTE. Generally, income from investments; specifically in this essay, income from investment in government debt. To circumvent the Catholic Church's opposition to lending money at interest, the French Crown raised loans by selling *rentes* or annuities. The *rente* (annuity or annual income) represented the interest on the capital surrendered by its purchaser to the government. That capital, which was never reimbursed, purchased either an annuity paid in perpetuity (*rente perpetuelle*) or an annuity paid during the lifetime of a named person, not necessarily the purchaser (*rente viagère*). The rate of interest represented by the *rente perpetuelle* was much more modest than that represented by the *rente viagère*.

TAILLE. The main direct tax under the Old Regime. In *pays de taille personelle* (the greater part of France) it was levied on 'common' persons, *taillables* (those liable to pay *taille*), i.e. peasants, according to presumed wealth. In *pays de taille réelle* (mainly in the south) it was levied on land deemed to be 'common' (listed as subject to *taille* in land registers), whether owned by nobles or commoners.

ULTRAMONTANISM. Literally, 'beyond the mountains', i.e. the Alps, an allusion to Italy and the papacy. An ecclesiastical ideology within the Catholic Church which exalted the authority of the Pope in doctrinal and disciplinary matters at the expense of bishops and secular Catholic rulers.

VENAL OFFICE. An office that could be purchased. Access to most offices in the royal administration (i.e. taxation, disbursement of revenue, justice) was by purchase, either from the government if the office had just been created, or from its existing owner if it was of long standing. Venal offices could be transmitted by inheritance as well as sold. Their holders were virtually unsackable because the government could only relieve them of their posts if it reimbursed the cost of their office. The more important venal offices conferred personal nobility on those who owned them and hereditary nobility if held by the same family over three generations.

VINGTIÈME. Literally, a twentieth. An attempt to tax all incomes regardless of status. The clergy secured exemption soon after its introduction in 1749 and the nobility tried to subvert the efficient assessment of income, but it was none the less one of the fairer taxes levied.

Further Reading

1. *Background Reading*

Alfred Cobban, *A History of Modern France, vol. 1: 1715–1799* (London, Penguin, first ed. 1957, 3rd 1968). Written before the reappraisal of the parlements, Necker and the crisis of 1787–8, but the only general survey of eighteenth-century France and very readable.

J.F. Bosher, *The French Revolution* (London, Weidenfeld and Nicolson, 1989). The first five chapters provide a valuable introduction to the society and institutions of the Old Regime and an account of its last years.

Simon Schama, *Citizens: A Chronicle of the French Revolution* (London, Viking, 1989). A long and colourful narrative and a great success with the general public. Over half is devoted to the background to the Revolution and the events of 1789.

2. *What was the Revolution?*

(i) The Marxist interpretation

Georges Lefebvre, *The Coming of the French Revolution*, translated by R.R. Palmer (Princeton, Princeton University Press, 1947). Essential to start with this classic account, an impressive and very readable synthesis. Written for the 150th anniversary of the Revolution in 1939, its destruction was ordered by the Vichy government.

(ii) Early challenges to the Marxist interpretation

Alfred Cobban, 'The myth of the French Revolution', in Alfred Cobban, *Aspects of the French Revolution* (London, Jonathan Cape, 1968), 90–111. Cobban was Professor of French History in the University of London (1954–68); this was his inaugural lecture.

Alfred Cobban, *The Social Interpretation of the French Revolution*

(London, Cambridge University Press, 1964). Not appreciated when it first appeared and in some respects overtaken by later research, but a pioneering achievement.

F. Crouzet, 'England and France in the eighteenth century: a comparative analysis of two economic growths', in R.M. Hartwell (ed.), *The Causes of the Industrial Revolution in England* (London, Methuen, 1967), 139–74. A classic essay, which stimulated research and debate by questioning the assumption that the French economy was retarded in the eighteenth century. Indispensable.

F. Crouzet, 'Criticisms and self-criticisms of a comparison', in F. Crouzet, *Britain Ascendant: Comparative Studies in Franco-British Economic History* (Cambridge, Cambridge University Press, 1990). Impressive survey of two decades' achievement in this field. A natural sequel to the foregoing.

George V. Taylor, 'Non-capitalist wealth and the origins of the French Revolution', *American Historical Review*, 72 (1967), 469–96. Very important: argues that, economically, the nobility and affluent middle class formed a single group.

(iii) On the nature and role of the nobility before the Revolution

Betty Behrens, 'Nobles, privileges and taxes in France at the end of the Ancien Regime', *Economic History Review*, 2nd series, 15 (1963), 451–75. Argues that the French nobility was one of the most heavily taxed in Europe. Challenged by G.J. Cavanaugh, 'Nobles, privileges and taxes in France. A revision reviewed', *French Historical Studies*, 8 (1974), 681–92. But see also the article by Peter Mathias and Patrick O'Brien on taxation in Britain and France listed below.

George V. Taylor, 'Types of capitalism in eighteenth-century France', *English Historical Review*, 79 (1964), 478–97. Argues (1) that these were very different from later industrial capitalism and (2) that some nobles were heavily involved therein.

Robert Forster, *The Nobility of Toulouse in the Eighteenth Century: A Social and Economic Study* (Baltimore, Johns Hopkins Press, 1960). Shows that they ran their estates with truly 'bourgeois' efficiency. Makes the same point in 'The noble wine producers of the Bordelais in the eighteenth century', *Economic History Review*, 2nd series, 14 (1961), 18–33, and in 'The provincial noble, a reappraisal', *American Historical Review*, 68 (1963), 681–91.

A. Goodwin, 'The social origins and privileged status of the French eighteenth-century nobility', *Bulletin of John Rylands Library*, 47 (1965), 382–403.

Roland E. Mousnier, *The Institutions of France under the Absolute Monarchy 1598–1789: Society and the State*, translated by Brian Pearce (Chicago, University of Chicago Press, 1979). Surveys the evolution of the nobility over a long period and within the context of the social structure as a whole.

Pierre Goubert, *The Ancien Regime: French Society, 1600–1750*, translated by Steve Cox (London, Weidenfeld and Nicolson, 1973). Lively, stimulating book, with documents. Like Mousnier, concludes that there was economic convergence between the wealthy nobility and bourgeoisie in the eighteenth century, but is much more readable.

Guy Chaussinand-Nogaret, *The French Nobility in the Eighteenth Century: From Feudalism to Enlightenment*, translated by William Doyle (Cambridge, Cambridge University Press, 1985). Vigorous statement of the 'new' view of the nobility, which stresses that it was constantly revitalized by an influx of wealth and talent from the bourgeoisie.

David D. Bien, 'Manufacturing nobles: the chancelleries in France to 1789', *Journal of Modern History*, 61 (1989), 445–486. Reinforces the conclusion that, for the wealthy, the means of access to the nobility were expanding, not contracting, in the eighteenth century.

Colin Lucas, 'Nobles, bourgeois and the origins of the French Revolution', *Past and Present*, 60 (1973), 84–126. Reprinted in D.W. Johnson (ed.), *French Society and the Revolution* (Cambridge, Cambridge University Press, 1976), 88–131. A very influential essay, which presents the evidence in support of the view that the nobility and bourgeoisie formed a single dominant class.

Robert Darnton, 'The high Enlightenment and the low life of literature in pre-Revolutionary France', *Past and Present*, 51 (1971), 81–115. Reprinted in D.W. Johnson (ed.), *French Society and the Revolution* (Cambridge, Cambridge University Press, 1976), 53–87, and in Robert Darnton, *The Literary Underground of the Old Regime* (London, 1982), 1–40. Typically witty, thought-provoking essay from the leading authority on publishing and the professional life of writers.

William Doyle, 'Was there an aristocratic reaction in pre-Revolutionary France?', *Past and Present*, 57 (1972), 97–122. Reprinted in Douglas Johnson (ed.), *French Society and the Revolution* (Cambridge, Cambridge University Press, 1976), 3–28. Demonstrates that there was not, and that the nobility had always dominated state and society.

William Doyle, *Origins of the French Revolution* (Oxford, Oxford University Press, 1989). The 'revisionist' answer to Lefebvre's *The Coming of the French Revolution*. Starts with an excellent historiographical essay. In his own account of the origins, responds boldly to the logic of the (mainly) Anglo-American empiricist version of revisionism by concentrating on the final crisis of 1787–8 and its outcome in 1789.

William Doyle, 'Reflections on the classic interpretation of the French Revolution', *French Historical Studies*, 16 (1990), 743–9; Michel Vovelle, 'Reflections on the revisionist interpretation of the French Revolution', op.cit., 749–55; Colin Lucas, Lynn Hunt, and Donald Sutherland, 'Commentaries on the papers of William Doyle and Michel Vovelle', op.cit., 756–65. The annual conference of the American Historical Association held in 1989 devoted one of its sessions to a debate on 'The Origins of the French Revolution'. This is a record of the main contributions to the debate; it is disappointing compared with that on Furet's interpretation of the Revolution; see below.

(iv) The Tocqueville-Furet interpretation

François Furet, 'The Revolutionary catechism', in François Furet, *Interpreting the French Revolution*, translated by Elborg Forster (London, Cambridge University Press, 1981). This essay, first published in *Annales E.S.C.*, 27 (March–April 1971), 255–89, is a scathing attack on the leading exponents of the Marxist interpretation of the Revolution. An essay on Tocqueville appeared the same year in a *festschrift* for Raymond Aron and is also reprinted in *Interpreting the French Revolution*. There is much to be said for reading the essays in this order, before embarking on the first essay in this volume, 'The French Revolution is over'. (There is a fourth essay on Augustin Cochin, highly regarded by Furet at the time of writing, but not included in the *Critical Dictionary*.) As Lynn Hunt comments in her lucid review of the French edition [*History and Theory*, 20 (1981), 313–23], 'the prose is often maddeningly elusive, but the labour of reading is worth the effort'.

Tony Judt, *Marxism and the French Left: Studies in Labour and*

Politics in France 1830–1981 (Oxford, Clarendon, 1986), ch. 4, 'French Marxism 1945–75', considers the intellectual background to the renunciation of Marxism by leading French intellectuals, including Furet; a fascinating, witty account.

Alexis de Tocqueville, *The Old Régime and the Revolution*, translated by Stuart Gilbert (New York, Doubleday Anchor Books, 1955). Vital to an understanding of Tocqueville and Furet but not a reliable guide to the Old Regime.

François Furet and Mona Ozouf (eds.), *A Critical Dictionary of the French Revolution*, translated by Arthur Goldhammer (Cambridge, Mass., Belknap Press of Harvard University Press, 1989). A large collection of essays on various aspects of the Revolution — events, participants, institutions, ideas, historians and commentators — many of them written by the editors. The volume as a whole bears Furet's imprint: the origins of the Revolution (which do not interest him) are ignored and academic history (the dominant, post-1890 republican-Marxist tradition) is dismissed in one essay. The sixteen essays on the early historians and commentators are uneven in quality: those by Furet himself and Ozouf are stimulating.

Keith Michael Baker, *The French Revolution and the Creation of Modern Political Culture*, vol. 1: *The Political Culture of the Old Regime* (Oxford, Pergamon Press, 1987). A collection of conference papers, some in French, some in English, which reflect Furet's general view, that the Revolution was an episode in the political and cultural, not the social and economic, history of France. Review articles by Jack R. Censer, 'The coming of a new interpretation of the French Revolution?', *Journal of Social History*, 21 (1988), 295–309, and by Sarah Maza, 'Politics, culture, and the origins of the French Revolution', *Journal of Modern History*, 61 (December 1989), 704–23, help to place the conference and volume in their appropriate historiographical context.

Claude Langlois, 'Furet's Revolution', *French Historical Studies*, 16 (1990), 766–76; David D. Bien, 'François Furet, the Terror, and 1789', op.cit., 777–83; Donald Sutherland, 'An assessment of the writings of François Furet', op.cit., 784–91; François Furet, 'A commentary', op.cit., 792–802. These four papers were originally delivered to the American Historical Association's annual conference held in San Francisco in 1989 in a session devoted to 'François Furet's interpretation of the French Revolution'. They provide a critical but fair introduction to this controversial yet influential historian.

3. The Depredations of War and Debt

Paul Kennedy, *The Rise and Fall of the Great Powers* (London, Unwin Hyman, 1988). Ch. 3 is a good general introduction to the problems of war and finance in the eighteenth century.

Albert Sorel, *Europe and the French Revolution: The Political Traditions of the Old Régime*, translated and edited by Alfred Cobban and J.W. Hunt (London, Collins, 1969). A classic, published in 1885, the first volume (and the best) of an eight-volume study of the French Revolution in its European setting; contains a readable critical survey of French foreign policy during the Old Regime.

A.M. Wilson, *French Foreign Policy during the Administration of Cardinal Fleury, 1726–1743* (Cambridge, Mass., Harvard University Press, 1936; reprinted Greenwood Reprint, 1972). Excellent account of Fleury's achievement and of international relations in Europe in the first half of the eighteenth century.

J.O. Lindsay (ed.), *The New Cambridge Modern History, vol. VII: The Old Regime, 1713–63* (London, Cambridge University Press, 1970). Contains useful chapters on 'The War of Austrian Succession', by Mark A. Thomson (416–39), 'The Diplomatic Revolution', by D.B. Horn (440–64), and 'The Seven Years War', by Eric Robson (465–86).

James C. Riley, *The Seven Years War and the Old Regime in France: The Economic and Financial Toll* (Princeton, Princeton University Press, 1986). Important. Argues that the damage inflicted on French trade has been exaggerated and gives a detailed examination of the war's financial consequences.

Gabriel Ardant, 'Financial policy and economic infrastructure of modern states and nations', in *The Formation of National States in Western Europe*, ed. Charles Tilley (Princeton, Princeton University Press, 1975), 164–218. Unrivalled for its insight into the problems of government finance and taxation in the early modern period. A comparative study (by a former *inspecteur général des finances* and leading authority on taxation), but France is the main example discussed.

Peter Mathias and Patrick O'Brien, 'Taxation in Britain and France, 1715–1810. A comparison of the social and economic incidence of taxes collected for the central governments', *Journal of European Economic History*, 5 (1976), 601–50. Questions several generally accepted conclusions about French taxes, but needs to be read with critical attention to the authors' own caveats and qualifications.

Robert D. Harris, 'French finances and the American War, 1777–83', *Journal of Modern History*, 48 (1976), 233–58. Radical reappraisal of the traditional view that Necker's financing of the war by credit was unusual and irresponsible.

O.T. Murphy, *Charles Gravier, Comte de Vergennes: French Diplomacy in the Age of Revolution* (Albany, N.Y., State University of New York Press, 1982). Traditional diplomatic history, which contains a clear and useful chapter on the Diplomatic Revolution and is particularly relevant to an understanding of France's entry into the War of American Independence.

4. *The Crown, the Parlements and the Church*

(i) The 'refusal of sacraments' controversy and its implications

John McManners, 'Jansenism and politics in the eighteenth century', in *Church, Society and Politics*, ed. Derek Baker (Oxford, Blackwell, 1975), 253–73. Sharp, witty account of the bull *Unigenitus* and its ecclesiastical and political consequences.

B. Robert Kreiser, *Miracles, Convulsions and Ecclesiastical Politics in Early Eighteenth-Century Paris* (Princeton, Princeton University Press, 1978). First chapter gives a useful explanation of what is understood by Jansenism, Molinism, and Gallicanism.

Dale Van Kley, *The Jansenists and the Expulsion of the Jesuits from France 1757–1765* (New Haven and London, Yale University Press, 1975). Important study which demonstrates that a Jansenist 'party' within the Parlement of Paris was responsible for the campaign to expel the Jesuits. Also argues that the alliance between Jansenists and judges contributed to the success of enlightened values in France, not simply by destroying the one group in the Church best equipped to defend it intellectually against the *philosophes* (the established view), but also by propagating secularized versions of Jansenist principles which were radical and subversive of absolute monarchy.

Dale Van Kley, *The Damiens Affair and the Unravelling of the Ancien Régime, 1750–1770* (Princeton, Princeton University Press, 1984). The best account of the refusal of sacraments controversy, the

resulting struggle between Crown and parlements, and the development of the parlements' constitutional claims.

Dale Van Kley, 'Church, state and the ideological origins of the
French Revolution: the debate over the General Assembly of the
Gallican Clergy in 1765', *Journal of Modern History*, 51 (1979), 629–
66. Continues the story of the strife provoked by *Unigenitus*. Argues
that already by 1765 the divisions on political-ecclesiastical matters of
1789–91 were discernible in outline.

(ii) The struggle between Crown and parlements

A. Cobban, 'The Parlement of Paris in the eighteenth century',
History, 35 (1950), 64–80. Reprinted in A. Cobban, *Aspects of the
French Revolution* (London, Cape, 1968), 69–82. Lively statement of
the traditional view that the parlements were the grave-diggers of the
Old Regime.

J.H. Shennan, *The Parlement of Paris* (London, Eyre and Spottis-
woode, 1968). A major contribution to the reappraisal of the
parlements.

David Hudson, 'The parlementary crisis of 1763 in France and its
consequences', *Canadian Journal of History*, 7 (1972), 97–117. Argues
that success on ecclesiastical issues encouraged the parlements to
oppose the Crown more resolutely on fiscal matters during and at the
end of the Seven Years War, and that this in turn contributed to the
Crown's decision to crush the opposition of the parlements in 1770–1.

William Doyle, 'The Parlements of France and the breakdown of the
Old Regime, 1771–1788', *French Historical Studies*, 6 (1970), 415–58.
Challenges the traditional view, put forward by Cobban, that
Maupeou and Terray represented the last best chance of the Old
Regime. This account of the crisis of 1770–1 needs to be sup-
plemented with that of John Bosher, 'The French crisis of 1770',
History, 57 (1972), 17–30.

David Carl Hudson, 'In defense of reform: French government propaganda during the Maupeou crisis', *French Historical Studies*, 8
(1973), 51–76. Comes to the opposite conclusion from that of Doyle.

Durand Echeverria, *The Maupeou Revolution: A Study in the History
of Libertarianism: France 1770–1774* (Baton Rouge and London,
Louisiana State University Press, 1985). Mainly concerned with elu-
cidating the main strands in the debate that followed the reform of the
parlements, but begins with a good, brief account of Maupeou's coup.

William Doyle, *The Parlement of Bordeaux and the End of the Old Regime 1771–1790* (London, Benn, 1974). Concludes that the parlement was at its most effective in defending the interests of the province. Its opposition to the Crown on national issues was weakened by internal divisions dating from 1771 and memories of Maupeou's coup.

5. *The Failure of Reform*

(i) Reform ministers and reform projects

Douglas Dakin, *Turgot and the Ancien Régime in France* (London, Methuen, 1939). Admirable study. It gives a favourable and persuasive view of Turgot and a vivid impression of the difficulties under which he worked as a minister and an intendant.

Robert D. Harris, *Necker: Reform Statesman of the Ancien Régime* (Berkeley, California, University of California Press, 1979). Makes a powerful case in defence of Necker's first ministry. See also his article, 'Necker's *compte rendu* of 1781: a reconsideration', *Journal of Modern History*, 42 (1970).

Steven Kaplan, *Bread, Politics and Political Economy in the Reign of Louis XV* (2 vols. The Hague, Martinus Nijhoff, 1976). Important monograph on the first experiment in free trade in grain and its consequences.

J.F. Bosher, *The Single Duty Project: A Study of the Movement for a French Customs Union in the Eighteenth Century* (London, Athlone, 1964). Describes the attempts to introduce internal free trade and the reasons why they foundered.

John Bosher, *French Finances 1770–1795: From Business to Bureaucracy* (Cambridge, Cambridge University Press, 1973). Indispensable. Broke new ground by turning attention away from taxation to financial administration and control. In doing so, started the rehabilitation of Necker.

(ii) The Assembly of Notables and the crisis of 1787–8

A. Goodwin, 'Calonne, the Assembly of French Notables of 1787 and the origins of the "Revolte Nobiliaire"', *English Historical Review*, 61 (1946), 202–34, 329–77. The natural starting-point for any study of the Assembly of Notables. Goodwin was one of the first historians to take Calonne seriously as a reforming minister. However, the more favourable view that is currently taken of Necker (by Harris and Bosher, above) necessarily has the effect of undermining Calonne's reputation.

Jean Egret, *The French Pre-Revolution, 1787–1788*, translated by Wesley D. Camp (Chicago, University of Chicago Press, 1977). Indispensable. First published in France in 1962. Significant for the importance it attaches to contingency in what turned out to be the last crisis of the Old Regime. Also notable for its rehabilitation of Loménie de Brienne.

Vivian R. Gruder, 'Paths to political consciousness: the Assembly of Notables of 1787 and the "Pre-Revolution" in France', *French Historical Studies*, 13 (1984), 323–55, and 'A mutation in elite political culture: the French notables and the defense of property and participation, 1787', *Journal of Modern History*, 55 (1984), 598–634. Considers the impact of the Assembly of Notables on those who took part in it.

Dale Van Kley, 'The Jansenist constitutional legacy in the French Pre-Revolution, 1750–1789', *Historical Reflections*, 13 (1986), 393–453. Traces the continuing influence of Jansenist constitutional doctrine in the crisis of 1787–9.

Vivian R. Gruder, 'The Bourbon monarchy: reforms and propaganda at the end of the Old Regime', in Keith Michael Baker (ed.), *The Political Culture of the Old Regime* (Oxford, The Pergamon Press, 1987), 347–74. Considers the reform measures put to the Assembly of Notables and the Estates-General in the Royal Session of 23 June 1789. Also examines royalist propaganda, which sometimes exacerbated social divisions and polarized opinion.

6. *The Revolution becomes Radical*

(i) The struggle to gain control of the Estates-General

E.L. Eisenstein, 'Who intervened in 1788? A commentary on *The Coming of the French Revolution*', *American Historical Review*, 71 (1965), 77–103. Points out that the members of the privileged orders took the lead in the campaign to modernize the Estates-General.

J. Kaplow, 'Class in the French Revolution: on "Who intervened in 1788?" A discussion', *American Historical Review*, 72 (1967), 498–

522. A response to Eisenstein. This article, the following one in the same journal by Gilbert Shapiro, 'The many lives of Georges Lefebvre', 502–14, and Eisenstein's reply to Kaplow and Shapiro, 514–22, demonstrate the passion aroused by criticism of Lefebvre.

D. Wick, 'The court nobility and the French Revolution: the example of the Society of Thirty', *Eighteenth Century Studies*, 13 (1980), 263–84. Another analysis of the membership of the Society of Thirty reveals that a large proportion of them were disgruntled court aristocrats.

Robert D. Harris, *Necker and the Revolution of 1789* (Lanham, University Press of America, 1986). Detailed account of Necker's role.

Bronislaw Baczko, 'The social contract of the French: Sieyès and Rousseau', *Journal of Modern History*, 60 (Supplement), (1988), S98–S125. Discusses the development of the concepts of constituent power and representation in Sieyès's thought and their consequences for contemporaneous politics.

François Furet, 'The monarchy and the procedures for the elections of 1789', *Journal of Modern History*, 60 (Supplement) (1988), S58–S74. Argues that the electoral procedures, with their explosive mixture of antique and modern features, explain why absolute monarchy was replaced by democratic egalitarianism. A translation of Furet's contribution to the volume of Chicago conference papers edited by Keith Michael Baker (see above).

(ii) Popular insurrection

C.E. Labrousse, 'The crisis in the economy at the end of the Old Regime', in Ralph W.Greenlaw (ed.), *The Economic Origins of the French Revolution* (Boston, Heath, 1958), 59–72. A convenient summary in English of Labrousse's conclusion that the population was expanding more quickly than the economy in the eighteenth century.

G. Rudé, *The Crowd in the French Revolution* (Oxford, Clarendon Press, 1959). Highly-regarded study in its time. Chs.1–4 inclusive are still the best introduction to the popular insurrections in Paris in 1789.

Colin Lucas, 'The crowd in politics between *Ancien Régime* and Revolution in France', *Journal of Modern History*, 60 (1988), 421–57. Important. Questions the extent to which the action of the Paris crowd was prompted by political consciousness in 1789.

J. Godechot, *The Taking of the Bastille: July 14th, 1789*, translated by Jean Stewart (London, Faber and Faber, 1970). Useful account of the events of the summer in Paris.

Georges Lefebvre, *The Great Fear of 1789: Rural Panic in Revolutionary France*, translated by Joan White (London, New Left Books, 1973). Published in France in 1932, it quickly established itself as a classic.

P.M. Jones, *The Peasantry in the French Revolution* (Cambridge, Cambridge University Press, 1988). Admirable synthesis of recent research. Chs. 1–3 provide the best succinct account of the origins and outbreak of the peasant insurrection.

Index